*Monique Baqué*

*Pierre Baqué*

*Yves Becmeur*

*Sylvain Bernard*

*Jacques Cordeau*

*Henriette Gonse*

*Maurice Laroche*

*Hélène Mars*

*André Servois*

*Claude Troger*

# INTRODUCTION TO THE VISUAL ARTS

D1509286

*Under the Patronage of Jean Sauboa, Inspector General, Public Education, France*

*American Editor: S. Ralph Maurello, Director of Graphic Arts, State University College, Plattsburgh, New York*

## TUDOR PUBLISHING COMPANY
*New York*

# FOREWORD

## GENERAL CHARACTER OF THE BOOK

The text, limited to essentials, leaves a good deal of leeway for the teacher's own ideas and development. The illustrations have been carefully chosen to exemplify and expand upon the points made in the text. They constitute abundant documentation from the history of art, drawn from widely different periods and countries, and can be used as starting points for numerous exercises.

## PLAN OF THE BOOK

It is composed of four interdependent parts.

a) *Materials and means of expression.*

This section deals with the basic principles of such techniques as drawing, watercolor, scratchboard and linoleum block printing.

b) *Observation.*

This part is intended to teach the student to see and to analyze. It deals with such matters as the fundamental ideas of color, perspective, page layout, enveloping forms, proportions, and so on.

c) *Decoration.*

Richly illustrated, this section of practical and historical information is intended to facilitate, by means of images, the acquisition and comprehension of basic principles of design. It points up the existence and permanence of certain themes and constitutes a repertory of forms. It should permit a more penetrating analysis of works of art. Through information on such techniques as pottery and mosaic, it enters into the domain of practical, daily life.

d) *Imagination.*

Here, the student will have a chance to put the knowledge so far acquired to use in freer, more personal applications. This section thus provides the key to the world of poetry and fantasy.

The various sections are linked together by examples and by repeated demonstration of common laws (of design, composition, color harmony, etc.).

The link with other branches of art is implicitly contained in exercises in observation, decorative techniques, and the suggested topics and themes for drawing.

Treated in this manner, "practical art" becomes a true "introduction to the visual arts." It develops in the student special aptitudes for seeing, analyzing and judging with taste and discernment. Practical art thus takes its place harmoniously along with other branches of learning as a means of acquiring a general cultural background; and remains a permanent point of contact between life and works of the creative imagination.

THE AUTHORS

# TABLE OF CONTENTS

# I. EQUIPMENT.
# MEANS OF EXPRESSION

1. The transformation of a color (red).

2. The magic of the line. A witch.
Hieronymus Bosch (Louvre).

— Equipment.
— Using the pencil — the line.
— Using the pencil — surfaces.
— Using paints.
— Scratchboard, linoleum block prints, drawing with glue.

3. The word "paper" comes from "papyrus," the bark of a reed of the Nile, on which the Egyptians wrote. In the Middle Ages, parchment, specially treated lamb or goat skin, was used. Paper as we know it, made from rags, is a more recent invention. Today, paper is ordinarily made from wood. Papyrus. Egypt (Louvre).

# EQUIPMENT

The choice of materials is very important as the results are considerably influenced by it.

The greatest attention should be given to:

- Drawing paper
- Pencils
- Paints

## I — THE PAPER

In choosing drawing paper take into account:

• **Its color:** White paper is generally best for most exercises.

• **Its purpose:** Papers do not all serve the same purpose. A bond paper is suitable for pencil and chalk drawing. Charcoal paper and rough newsprint are good for charcoal and pastel drawing.

A medium weight vellum (70 lb.) or a 2-ply Bristol (kid finish) are good all-purpose papers.

A heavy rag paper (120 lb. or more), cold pressed, is used for transparent watercolor.

Gouache or poster color can be used on any fairly heavy paper.

• **Its form:** Paper may be purchased in sheets, rolls, package or pad form. Sheets or pads 9"x12" in size are useful. Watercolor paper should be larger; 19"x24" is a good size. So-called "student grade" paper is less expensive than professional grade.

## II — PENCILS

The most commonly employed are black-lead or graphite pencils (fig. 4).

The hardness of the lead varies, and each brand offers a large choice, such as the following:

| Very Hard | Hard | Medium | Soft | Very Soft |
|-----------|------|--------|------|-----------|
| 9H | 2H HF No. 3 | HB No. 2 | B 2B No. 1 | 6B |

It is not necessary to have the complete series; two pencils from the medium group are perfectly satisfactory.

Example: hard lead: 2H or H;

          soft lead: B.

Since the pencil HB has the qualities of both groups it can very well replace pencil B or pencil H.

To avoid errors in gradation it is a good idea to pick two pencils of the same brand.

## III — PAINTS

**1. Gouache** and **watercolor:** these paints are soluble in water and consist of a mixture of colored pigment and gum.

Watercolor gives very transparent tones; gouache (or poster color) is opaque and coats.

**2.** Presentation (fig. 5):

— Watercolor: paints in cups;
                small tubes.

— Gouache:    paints in cups;
                larger-sized tubes; jars.

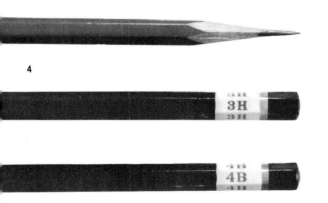

4

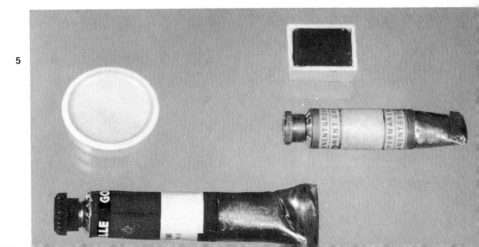

5

**6**

A more or less complete selection of colors can be found in most good quality paint boxes. The choice of colors is very important and the following list is a "minimum palette" (fig. 6):

- Purplish-blue: ultramarine;
- Greenish-blue: prussian blue, cerulean blue, turquoise.
- Purplish-red: carmine, alizarin crimson;
- Yellowish-red: vermilion;
- Orangish-yellow: Cadmium yellow;
- Greenish-yellow: lemon yellow.

Supplementary colors may be added, such as:

- Viridian (green);
- Yellow ocher;
- Burnt sienna;
- Violet.

In any case, this list must be completed with:

- Black;
- White (in a larger quantity for gouache because it is used in many mixtures).

**3.** Brushes (fig. 7):

- Two supple brushes of marten, squirrel, or sable, etc., and of different sizes, are sufficient (No. 6 and No. 12, for example).
- A flat, stiff bristle brush of medium size (No. 10, for example) will be needed for some exercises in gouache.

## IV — ADDITIONAL EQUIPMENT

- Portfolio and clips;
- Soft eraser (preferably with beveled ends);
- Soft sponge;
- Small roller for use in gouache backgrounds;
- Scissors (fig. 8).

**7**

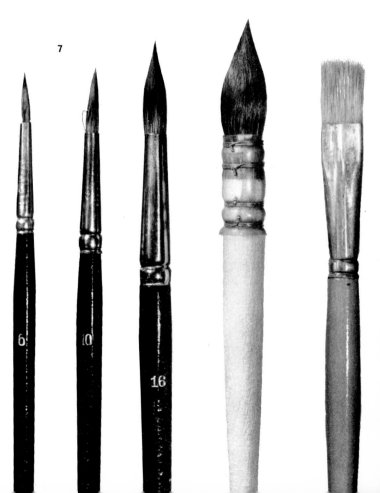

8

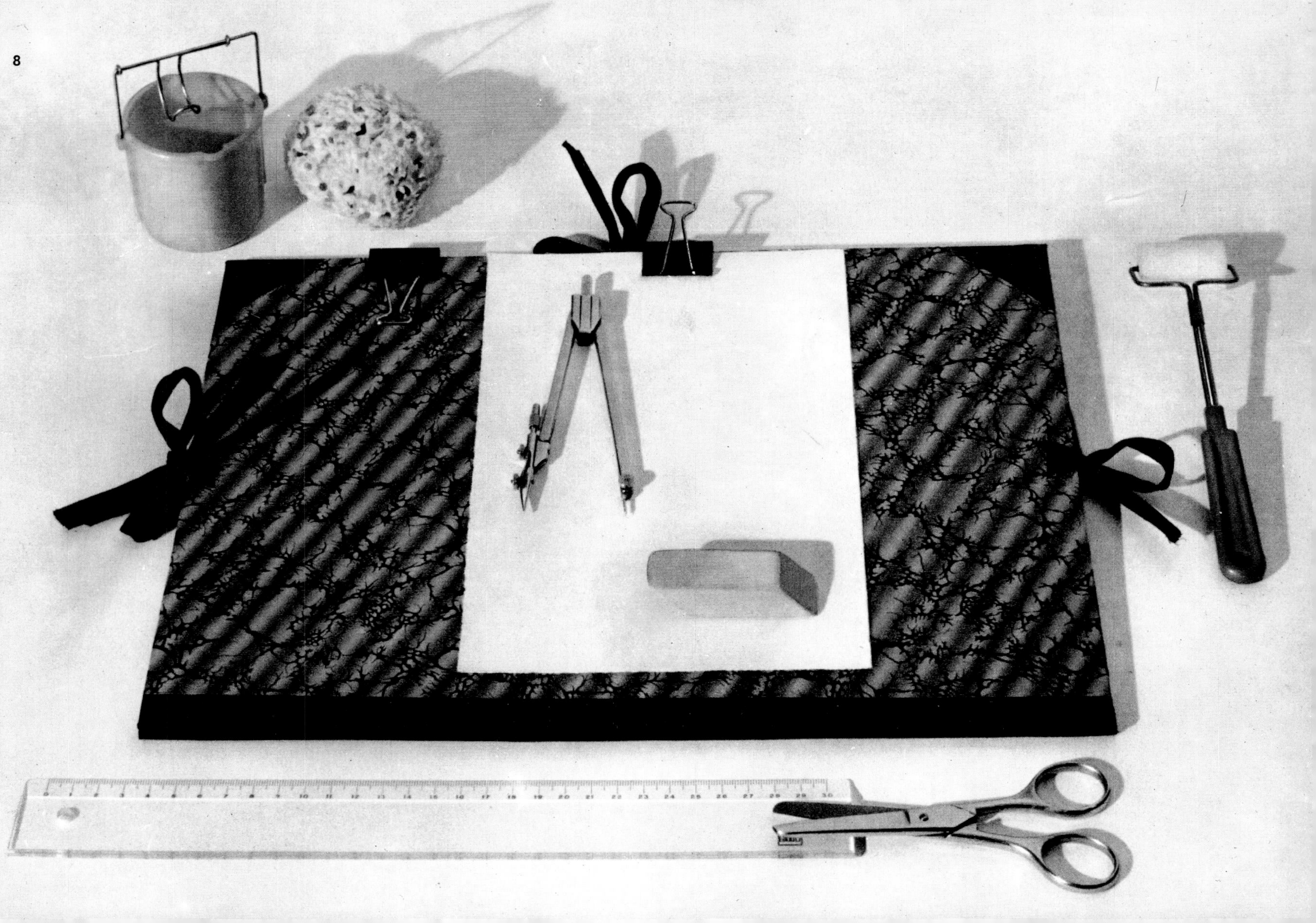

# USING THE PENCIL — THE LINE

## I — DRAWING A STRAIGHT LINE FREEHAND — THE PLAIN LINE

To draw a straight line freehand:

• Divide the distance to be covered into several segments and mark with dots for guides.

• Make several practice strokes without putting the pencil on the paper. This back-and-forth motion from one dot to another, repeated several times, gives the hand more assurance.

• Draw the line by segments, without bearing down and being careful to maintain the same thickness throughout (especially at the dots).

• Practice staying at the same distance from the edge of the page (or from a ruler-drawn line).

## II — THE "SHADED," "GRADATED," OR "MODULATED" LINE

Its thickness varies; it includes:

— Dark, wide sections: the "full" or heavy stroke;
— Light, slender sections: the light stroke.

The shaded or modulated line can express:

**1. Distance in space:**

As a general rule, intensity decreases with distance. Strokes delineating the contours of branches, for example, should be more vigorous and darker for the foreground parts, more attenuated and lighter for those in the background.

**2.** The edges of zones of **shade** and **light:**

A thick, dark stroke describes the contours of regions situated in the shade, while a slender, pale stroke is used for those in lighted regions.

**3.** Differences in **color:**

A fine gray line is used for the contours of a lemon-yellow ribbon; a thicker, darker line for the outline of an ultramarine ribbon.

9. In this bas-relief contours become thicker in the shade and thinner in the light. Basalt stele, Mexico, 1324-1521 A. D. (Museum of Anthropology, Mexico).

10. The drawn line emphasizes the articulations and suggests volume. Cow. Pisanello (Louvre).

Note:

— When employing the shaded line always define the contours first with a light line, which can then be retouched and accented.

**4.** Differences in **substance:**

A fine, light line expresses the transparency of a dragonfly's wing, while a thicker, more vigorous stroke will forcefully express the roughness of tree bark.

**5.** The articulation of **volumes,** or the more important parts:

Generally speaking, an "accentuation" or an "accent" is used to bring out a detail when the latter is particularly charactistic:

Examples: In a study of branches: to accentuate the joints of the branches, the nodes;

In a study of birds: to accentuate the head and feet (characteristic elements of their way of life).

11. The drawn line expresses the textures of the coats. Goat and lamb. Pisanello (Louvre).

13. The quality of the line is not the same for the face, the hands, the dress and the accessories. Madame X. Ingres (Private collection, Paris).

## III — USES — ADVANTAGES AND DISADVANTAGES OF THE PLAIN LINE AND THE MODULATED LINE

1. The plain line: equal width throughout.
   — It is neat, precise and clear.
   — For this reason it is used in industrial design (fig. 12), blueprints, dimensioned sketches, scientific diagrams, and architectural layouts.
   — However, it can appear dull, monotonous or lifeless.

2. The modulated line: varying in width.
   — It is richer, more expressive, more alive.
   — It is used in nature sketches, in life studies and in illustrations.

   Whether plain or modulated the line is also a principal means of graphic expression in decorative design (see p. 97).

12. Side view plan of a truck.

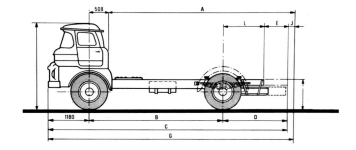

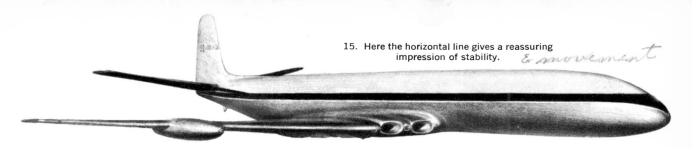

15. Here the horizontal line gives a reassuring impression of stability. *& movement*

14. Vertical lines can express immobility and nobility. King Solomon. Notre-Dame de Corbeil (Louvre).

## THE LINE AS A MEANS OF EXPRESSION

16. Vertical and horizontal lines create an atmosphere of balance, calm, and simplicity. Interior. Peter de Hooch (Wallace Coll., London).

18. The curved line expresses suppleness, life, gracefulness and sometimes movement. Sarasvati (Calcutta).

17. Eero Saarinen has purposely emphasized the functional obliqueness of the pillars to give more dynamism to his architecture (Dulles Airport, Washington).

19. The exclusive use of straight lines creates an impression of lifelessness. Monotony and boredom emanate from the façade of this housing project.

20. The excessive use of curved lines can result in a lack of vigor. Balcony in Art Nouveau style, Paris.

The judicious combination of straight and curved lines creates balanced, harmonious ensembles.

# USING THE PENCIL — SURFACES

To represent thoroughly with a pencil the volume of an object by the play of light and shadow, to express certain contrasts of color, value or substance, the line, even modulated, is not sufficient. One needs "grays," varying in darkness, both flat and shaded.

## I — HOW TO OBTAIN A FLAT GRAY WITH A PENCIL ON A GIVEN SURFACE

A sharp pencil is used on a fairly fine-grained paper.

The area to be covered is first outlined with fine lines.

Then a scumble is begun by moving the lead back and forth regularly over the paper. The first effort ordinarily produces a more or less uneven gray, usually too light in tone. To correct these defects repeat the operation several times until a flat, uniform gray of the desired intensity is obtained. At this stage, the original guide lines will no longer be visible.

The most difficult part of the procedure is to remain within the limits of the area to be covered; with perseverance and practice, though, it soon becomes easy (fig. 23A).

Note:
- The largest dimension of the surface to be covered (or the direction of the form) determines the direction of the pencil strokes (fig. 21).
- The use of the stump is not recommended for beginners; too often the results are only "dirty" and lifeless grays.

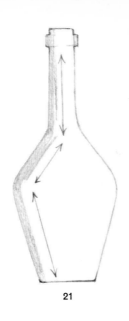

21

22. Drawing. Seurat (De Frenne Collection, Paris).

23 A

23 B

## II — HOW TO OBTAIN A SHADED GRAY

Begin with the portion which is to be the darkest, using an HB or No. 2B pencil. Bear down hard enough so that the lead "takes" on the paper, going over the area several times if necessary.

Then, progressively moving on to lighter parts, let the pencil touch the paper more and more lightly. The gray should fade evenly and gradually (figs. 22 and 23B).

24. Watercolor. Aujame.

# USING PAINTS

As in other types of art, the results here depend on the personal qualities of the individual, but these cannot be developed without a thorough knowledge of the various techniques and their possibilities. Watercolor does not produce the same effects as gouache, and the procedures are very different as well. Anyone who is unaware of this will have a long struggle before being able to control his efforts.

## I — WATERCOLOR

**1.** Consistency of the paint:

A small quantity of paint is generously diluted with water to make a very fluid colored liquid.

**2.** Procedure:

The watercolor paper (or heavy drawing paper) may be dampened with a soft sponge before being used. The paint, applied with a supple brush, spreads out within the outlines of the design. Adjoining colors often fuse to give new mixtures.

Blank parts of the paper are reserved to express the palest values.

**3.** Characteristics:

The transparency and luminosity of the paint gives the watercolor drawing a special freshness. This is the principal advantage of this technique (fig. 24).

**4.** Disadvantages:

The characteristic freshness disappears with retouching, when one color is painted over another. Of course, interesting results and delicate nuances can be obtained by superimposing colors, but these require a great deal of practice and real sensitivity.

**5.** Uses:

Nature sketches, landscapes, illustration.

## II — GOUACHE

**1.** Consistency of the paint:

The paint should be thicker than watercolor. The proportion of water is less and the consistency of the mixture should be like cream.

**2.** Procedure:

On thick, dry drawing paper, apply a good coat of paint in firm strokes. Paler tones are obtained by adding white.

**3.** Characteristics:

Gouache has a dull, sometimes thick appearance. The paper is not visible beneath.

**4.** Advantages:

The coating power of gouache permits easy retouching; new paint applied over dry paint hides the latter completely. Because of this facility, it is ideal for classroom use.

**5.** Uses:

Observation studies, decorative design, imaginative drawings.


## III — THE PALETTE AND THE MIXTURES

The quantities of color, squeezed from the tubes, are placed around the outer edge of the palette. Mixing is done in the center, by successively adding colors, while carefully controlling the consistency of the mixture.

## IV — THE LINE

It is drawn with the tip of the brush, held vertically, perpendicular to the paper. The wrist should be bent to immobilize the forearm, the work carried out by the flexion of the fingers. One can also support the hand with the little finger outstretched or on a drawing rule which is moved during the work.

It is difficult to maintain the same width throughout; at joinings there is often an increase in width. The ideal would thus be to draw the line in one stroke. Here again, practice plays a large role.


## V — THE SURFACE

**1.** Plain color:

• **Small surface** (two or three inches square): the outer edges are painted first and the center section afterwards. The position of the brush is important: it should be inclined toward the interior of the surface to be covered (fig. 25).

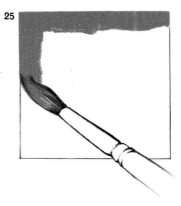

25

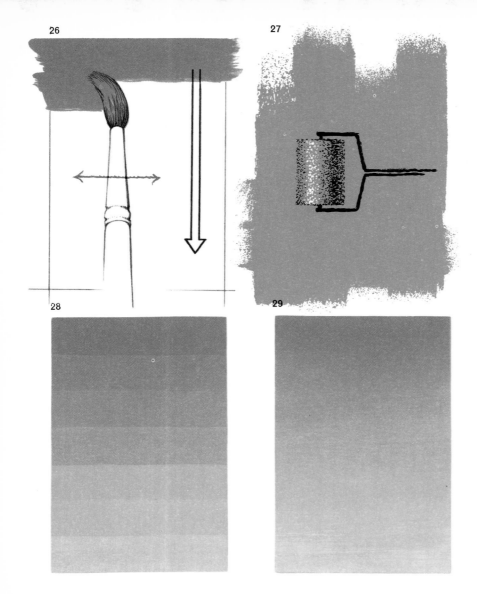

**• Large surface: the background:**

a) With a brush: dampen the paper with clean water. Using a large brush full of the chosen color, sweep the sheet horizontally from top to bottom; this must be done quickly so that each band of color blends partially into the preceding. The work is simpler when the outside limits of the area do not have to be precise (a "clean edge" can be obtained with masking tape, or the painted surface can be cut afterwards to the desired dimensions) (fig. 26).

b) With a roller a completely even background is **easily** obtained, by crisscrossing the bands (fig. 27).

**2.** Graded wash:

**• Graded wash with visible bands:**

Beginning at the top of the page and using a brush, paint a horizontal band of a dark color. Then add a little white to the original color to obtain a lighter tone and paint a second band absolutely flush with the first.

A little more white is added for the third; thus, from the top to the bottom the sheet is progressively covered with graded wash bands which evolve from the darkest shade of a color to the lightest (fig. 28).

**• Graded wash with invisible bands** (fig. 29):

The principle is the same, but the execution is more difficult as the separation between the horizontal bands of different tones should no longer be apparent; the result should be a progressive passage from one tone to the next. Among the different methods possible, the following may be chosen. We shall apply it here in a concrete example: a graded wash shading-off from black to white (fig. 30):

18

— Incline the paper and dampen it slightly with a sponge;

— At the top, paint a first horizontal band of pure black;

— Add a little white to the black paint; with the gray obtained, which is still very dark, make a second band of the same width, slightly overlapping the first;

— With a second clean, damp brush sweep the section between the two tones from left to right, several times if need be, so that the two colors blend;

— Add a little white to the gray and with the lighter tone paint a third band, always of the same width, slightly overlapping the second; again brush the "passage" between the two tones with a clean, damp brush;

— Repeat this operation with progressively lighter tones until pure white is reached.

— To be successful the work must be done rapidly while the paint is still wet so that each tone blends with the preceding. The paint must also be able to be spread well beyond the outline; here again masking tape can be used, or the painted sheet can be cut afterwards to the chosen dimensions.

30. These shadings are done in gouache. With watercolor the lighter tones are obtained by adding water.

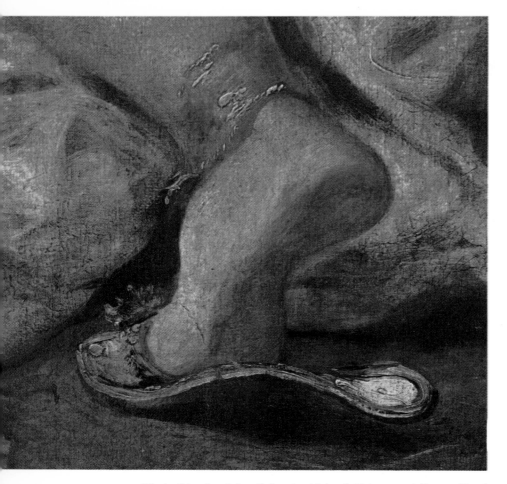

32. In this oil painting Delacroix obtains light tones and the sparkle of brilliant substances by scumbling and impasto. Similar results can be obtained in gouache by using the same method. The Death of Sardanapalus (detail). Delacroix (Louvre).

## VI — SCUMBLING OR DRYBRUSH

In the two procedures studied so far, plain color or graded wash, the paper itself was not visible through the paint. This is not true of drybrush, a technique which can be used effectively with gouache.

**1.** The tool:

A stiff bristle brush, preferably.

**2.** The support:

Perfectly **dry** paper, with more or less of a grain.

**3.** Procedure:

The tip of the brush is dipped in paint and the excess brushed off on another piece of paper. Brush the surface to be painted very lightly. The paint will be applied evenly in "granulations," but without hiding the paper, which should show through everywhere.

The finish obtained is rough (fig. 31).

**4.** Uses:

— Documentary studies: to render textures (feathers, tree bark, etc.);

— Still-lifes: to depict the sparkle of an object (fig. 32);

— Decoration: treatment of materials (stained-glass windows, ceramics . . .).

31

# SCRATCHBOARD, LINOLEUM BLOCK PRINTS, DRAWING WITH GLUE

## SCRATCHBOARD

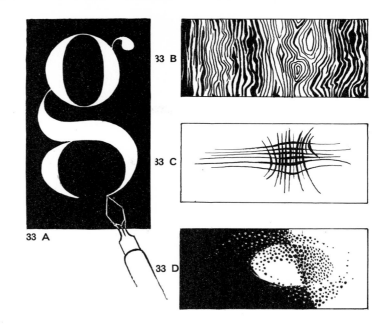

### THE SUPPORT

This is white, rather thick clay-coated cardboard created for this purpose, which one covers partially or totally with an even coat of India ink.

It can also be bought pre-coated with black ink.

Scratchboard technique is excellent for minute, precise work.

### THE TOOL

Any sharp point is suitable, but scratchboard pens and holders are available, and give very good results.

### PRINCIPLE

**1.** Line designs on **black scratchboard** (fig. 33A):

The point, when scratched against the India ink surface, uncovers the white backing; each stroke leaves a trace of white standing out on a black background, like a photographic negative.

**Retouching is possible:** errors can be covered up with a new application of India ink.

This method is ideal for outline drawing. One has only to sketch, preferably with a white pencil, the design to be scratched, or to transfer a design already prepared on tracing paper.

**2.** Design in values on a **white scratchboard:**

Surfaces of different shades, ranging from plain black to plain white, and passing through the intermediary grays, may be obtained by:

— **Crosshatching lines,** more or less close together, of white on black, varying in width, parallel or crossed (figs. 33B and C);

— White **dots** on a black surface or black on white (fig. 33D).

In this case it is preferable to work on a white scratchboard. The India ink is applied only to those parts which will eventually be black or gray; the white areas are not touched.

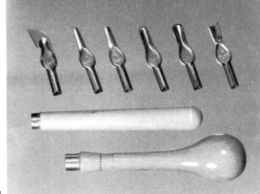

34

35

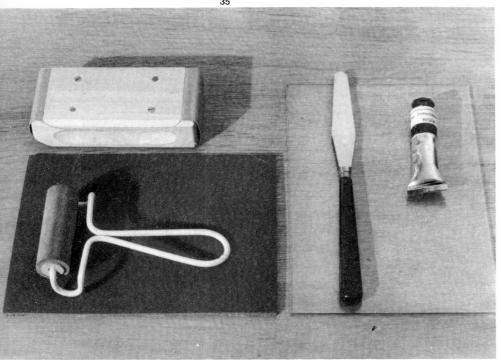

# LINOLEUM BLOCK PRINTS

## EQUIPMENT

**1.** Thick linoleum in pieces measuring 4"x5" or 5"x7", mounted on a burlap backing.

**2.** The cutting tools: these have sharp tips like chisels and are called "gouges." The tips are attached to short wooden handles, either straight or with rounded ends (fig. 34).

These tools are classified according to their shape into three groups:

a) The knife: used to cut the linoleum to the desired dimensions;

b) V-shaped gouges to cut the surface of the linoleum, making a triangular groove;

c) U-shaped gouges of varying widths to remove large surfaces.

**3.** The inking materials:

Letter press ink which is thick and spreads evenly over a glass plate with a rubber ink roller (fig. 35).

**4.** The paper:

Japanese rice paper is best, but lightweight bond paper gives good results; it can be found in white or slightly tinted.

## PROCEDURE

• The subject is drawn on the smooth side of the linoleum.

• With the gouges, the linoleum is hollowed out in all sections which are not to be inked, areas to appear white in the print. However, great care must be taken to reserve unmarked the exact areas which are to be coated with ink to reproduce the design (fig. 36).

• When the design is completed the linoleum is ready to be inked. The ink is spread on the glass plate; the roller, when run over this surface, picks up an even coat of ink and is then rolled over the linoleum. All the uncarved parts standing out are thus covered with a thin film of ink.

• The paper to be printed should be slightly dampened by contact with a moist blotter. It is now placed on the linoleum and covered with a thin sheet of cardboard. Pressure is applied evenly by means of a wooden roller moved over the cardboard's entire surface. The ink from the linoleum makes an imprint on the paper.

**The original design on the linoleum is done in reverse.** Thus, in some cases it is necessary to prepare the design on tracing paper and then turn it over.

The first imprint is usually a trial one; the ink must then be wiped off the linoleum and certain details of the design altered with the gouge before making new prints, until all details are perfectly clear (fig. 37).

> The linoleum must be inked before each printing, and on completion of the work the ink roller and the linoleum should be cleaned with turpentine or kerosene for future use.

Other possibilities for inking:

> colored inks;
>
> gouache plus a wetting agent.

36. The figure 4 is dug out from the linoleum in reverse.

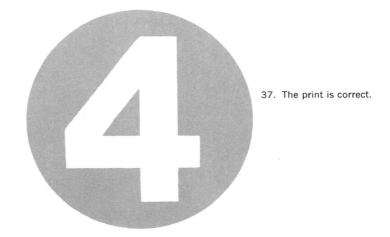

37. The print is correct.

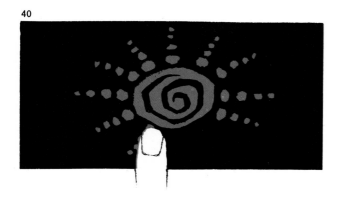

# GLUE PAINTING (RESIST)

## SUPPORT

An ordinary white or colored sheet of drawing paper.

## PROCEDURE

**1.** Drawing with glue (fig. 38):

A design is traced on paper with a brush, a pen or any other means, using liquid glue as if it were ordinary ink.

**2.** The background (fig. 39):

Over the entire surface of the page, including the design, a coat of gouache or ink is spread, of different tone or color than the paper. The design in glue is no longer visible.

**3.** The "resist" (fig. 40):

The surface is rubbed with the finger. The glue comes off easily, and the paper, formerly covered with glue, reappears, standing out against a background of gouache or ink.

A few minutes' wait is necessary between each operation to ensure complete dryness.

41. Child taking measurements. ▶

"When your hand and judgment are well trained you will draw quickly." Leonardo da Vinci.

42. Woods in the mist.

43. Rust and sky: complementary colors.

44. Plexiglass cubes.

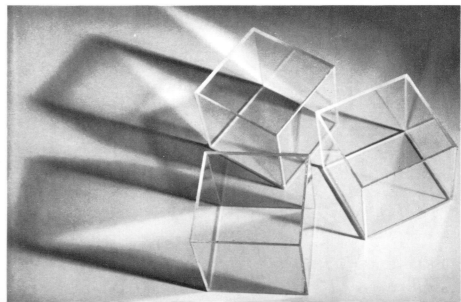

# 2. OBSERVATION

45. Dead bird. Dürer.

46. Bronze mortar (17th century).

# BASIC ASPECTS
## VALUES — COLORS

## OBSERVATION — VALUES

## I — THE SCALE OF TONES OR VALUES

In the above landscape, white corresponds to the light tone, gray to the medium tone, and black to the darkest tone. The three together constitute a **scale of tones or values;** between the black and the white, the extreme values, there exists theoretically an infinity of more or less dark grays, of more or less deep intermediate values (fig. 47).

48. Saint Matthew (detail). Rembrandt (Louvre).

## II — SHADE AND LIGHT

A quick examination of this landscape leads to the discovery of precise principles which are also easily found on a statue or on any other monochrome object illuminated by a spotlight.

This visual analysis is still easy when one examines a painting by Rembrandt or Georges de La Tour. The effect is created by a strong contrast between light and dark values; the principal subject, starkly illuminated, emerges from the shadows of varying degrees covering a large part of the picture. **The conception of value is closely related to that of shade and light** (figs. 48 and 49).

28

# III — VALUES AND COLORS

On the other hand, if one studies a painting by Bonnard or Claude Monet, one finds that the distinguishing of values is much more difficult. The objects stand out from one another by the play of colors, warm or cold, pure or mixed, and much more rarely by the contrast between light and dark tones.

A "black-and-white" photograph of the same picture proves to us that the scale of values does not go from pure white to pure black as in the Breughel landscape or the works of Georges de La Tour or Rembrandt.

This scale is established around numerous and very similar grays. To discover these slight differences, one must squint a little to eliminate the details and obtain an over-all view which reveals the almost imperceptible contrasts in value.

**The notion of value is linked to that of color,** but in a more complex way (figs. 50 and 51).

50 & 51. Landscape with Tugboat. Bonnard (Museum of Modern Art, Paris). In this landscape color is indispensable in order to identify the elements in the composition: lawn, trees, river, tugboat.

49. Saint Joseph Carpenter (detail).
Georges de la Tour (Louvre).

52

To draw a person, an animal, or an object, one can indicate:

— **The outline,** which defines the form;

— **The shadows and lights,** which express volume.

Color, although it gives a closer portrayal of reality, is not indispensable for visual comprehension of the world around us (examples: photographs, films, black-and-white television).

One might think that values (shadow and light) are not essential either, since the dimensioned sketch, for example, is composed only of lines. However, certain outlines are not always enough to express the third dimension.

### IV — VALUES OBSERVED IN SPACE

In this view (fig. 52), where the sky corresponds to the lightest value, one notices that the roofs are often darker in the foreground and that the contrast they make with the sky diminishes the farther away they are in space.

Painters have often employed this rule to create an illusion of depth. For this reason Vermeer often places in the foreground of his indoor compositions a dark curtain or a chair which creates an impression of depth, and behind which he paints in lighter values the personages or objects situated farther back in the room.

**The notion of value is linked to that of distance.**

53

For example, without shadow the sphere or the cone seen from above is merely a circle (fig. 53).

Shadow on the object itself is called **shade.**

The shadows which the lighted object casts are called **cast shadows.**

The shadow which a part of the object casts on another part of the same object is called a **self-cast shadow.**

### CONCLUSION

Thus we can say that the aspects of value or tone are linked with those of shade and light, color, and distance.

Artists have not always made use of shade (Egyptians, Greeks, Chinese, etc.).

Shade, a much more important factor in realism than color, appeared later in painting.

## GENERAL REMARKS

If an object is placed on a stool and brightly illuminated, one notices that:

— The shade and the cast shadow are situated on the side opposite the source of light (fig. 54);

— In the shade, in spite of the dark value, details remain visible (fig. 55);

— It is at the juncture of the light zone and the dark zone that details, whether in relief or sunken, are the most apparent; this juncture, called the "separator of shade and light," corresponds in its outline to the general form of the object. Even by itself it clearly reveals the form (fig. 56).

— Cast shadows are darker than shade (fig. 55).

The vase (fig. 54) is composed of volumes such as parallelepipeds, conic sections, portions of spheres and cylinders, all of which fit together to create a complex form whose arrangement of values is visible, but which is difficult to study. The analysis would be easier if the simple, geometric forms could be isolated and studied separately.

54. Plaster vase.

55. Ceramic bowls. 9th century, Iran (Foroughi Collection, Teheran).

56. Ceramic jar. 7th century B.C. Iran (Museum of Archeology, Teheran).

**31**

Middle tone — Light — Transition — Shade — Reflection

**57 A**

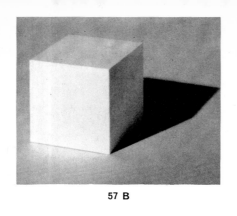

**57 B**

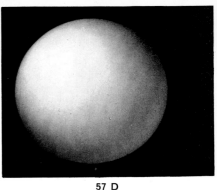

**57 C**

**57 D**

**Observation of shadows on the principal isolated forms:**

| | |
|---|---|
| 1. cube | half-tones |
| 2. cylinder | lights |
| 3. cone | shadows |
| 4. sphere | reflections |
| | transitions (fig. 57) |

*Remarks*

- **The character of the shadows depends upon the lighting:**

  Direct lighting → sharp shadows (projector, sun);
  Indirect lighting → softer shadows (filtered daylight, cloudy weather).

- **The character of the shadows depends on the color and value of the object lighted:**

  Light blue draperies → very visible shadows;
  Dark blue draperies → less visible shadows.

- **The character of the shadows depends on the material:**

  Brilliant object → sharp shadows and strong reflections;
  Dull object → more "enveloped" shadows and softer reflections (fig. 58).

## TO RENDER SHADE AND LIGHT

- **With pencil:** Surfaces receiving the light should be left blank (white paper);

  Surfaces in the shade should be rendered with more or less dark gray (see p. 15).

- **With paint:** Moderately lighted surfaces should be represented by a medium tone or local color (in principle, the brightest);

  Surfaces receiving the light by a middle tone plus white.

  Surfaces in shade by the medium tone plus the complementary color.

**58 A**

**58 B**

32

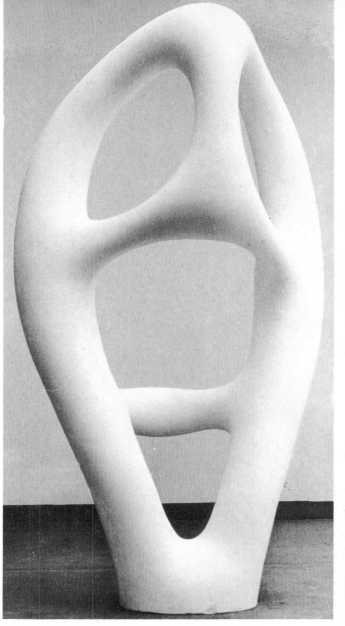

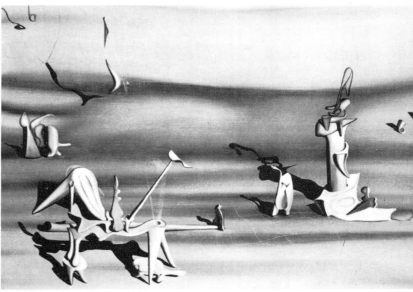

59. Sculpture. Ptolemy III. Jean Arp (Museum of Modern Art, Paris).

60. Tanguy makes use of cast shadows to emphasize the strange appearance of the forms. Day of Slowness (detail) (Museum of Modern Art, Paris).

61. Spherical reservoir at Lacq, France.

62. The prism separates white light into seven colors: red, orange, yellow, green, blue, indigo, violet. Spectrum (For the painter, indigo is only a shade of violet).

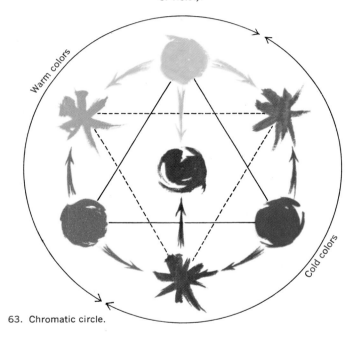

63. Chromatic circle.

64. In practice, secondary colors are brighter when certain shades of primary colors are used; thus, a mixture of tyrian rose (a purplish shade of red) and ultramarine blue gives a very luminous violet.

# ELEMENTARY PRINCIPLES
# OF COLOR

## THE CHROMATIC CIRCLE

### I — THE PRIMARY COLORS

The **three primary colors** are red, yellow, blue.

These are **basic** colors; they cannot be obtained by mixing other colors.

### II — SECONDARY COLORS

The **three secondary colors** are obtained by mixing the primary colors in pairs:

— yellow + red → orange
— yellow + blue → green
— red + blue → purple

### III — THE CHROMATIC CIRCLE

If one places:

— the primary colors at the points of an equilateral triangle, and

— the secondary colors at the points of a second triangle inverted on the first, thus forming a six-pointed star, one can trace a circle around the tips of the star: this is the **chromatic circle** (from the Greek *chroma* = color).

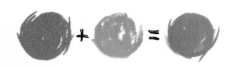  

# IV — THE COMPLEMENTARY COLORS

• **Remark:** two **complementary** colors are two colors diametrically opposite on the chromatic circle.

• **Definition:** blue, a primary color, is said to be the complement of orange (yellow + red), a secondary color, because it is not used in the mixture which produces orange. Thus, a primary color is the complement of the secondary color in which it does not occur.

For the same reason, a secondary color is the complement of the primary color which is not used in its composition.

Example: orange (yellow + red), a secondary color, is the complement of blue, a primary color.

65. The "three finger experiment": the index finger, dipped in yellow and rubbed against the middle finger, dipped in red, gives orange (yellow + red), complementary color of blue, covering the thumb. The blue completes the orange (yellow + red) to reconstitute the initial grouping of three primary colors.
The same experiment can be made for the other two pairs of complementary colors.

# V — WARM COLORS AND COLD COLORS

• "Warm" colors are red, yellow, orange (and their derivatives) (fig. 66).

• "Cold" colors are blue, green, violet (and their derivatives).

**Remarks:**

The distinction between warm colors and cold colors is, in reality, much more complex. A lemon yellow, for example, can be considered a "cold" yellow (it borders on green, a cold color). On the other hand, a golden yellow (bordering on orange) is a "warm" yellow.

66. Warm colors: Evocation of the Burgundy vineyards in autumn. Tapestry by Tourlière (La Demeure).

# THE CHROMATIC CIRCLE (Continued)

## PROPERTIES OF COMPLEMENTARY COLORS—SHADES

### I — PROPERTIES OF COMPLEMENTARY COLORS

**1.** Two complementary colors form a contrast:

- **The juxtaposition of two complementary colors makes each appear brighter.**

  Example: A red seems to have more color, more brightness when it is placed beside a green than beside any other color (fig. 67).

67

- **The principle of "simultaneous" contrast:** any color tends to color the adjoining space with its complementary color.

  Examples: Purple placed next to white gives it a yellowish cast (fig. 68);

  Red placed next to white makes it appear greenish (fig. 68):

  Yellow placed next to blue does not have the same aspect as yellow placed next to red (fig. 69);

  In summer a tan appears deeper when one wears light blue (or lavender) clothing.

68

69

- **The principle of successive contrast:** If, after staring for a minute or two at a red object, one then looks at a white surface, the form of the object is projected, but in green.

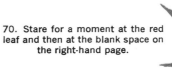

70. Stare for a moment at the red leaf and then at the blank space on the right-hand page.

- **Note:** one should avoid putting two complementary colors side by side, particularly when they are bright and of the same texture. The resulting contrast is tiring to the eyes.

However, in some cases, the contrast of complementaries is useful; in advertising, for example, a color-contrasted poster "catches" the eye.

**2.** Two complementary colors mixed together form a "gray"; i.e., they neutralize each other.

"Complementary couples abolish each other as colors when their diametric blending ends in gray"                                    Klee.

(For the physicist, the mixture of two complementary colored lights produces white.)

## II — SHADES

Definition:

One calls the shade of a color the variation of that color when it is mixed with a small quantity of a neighboring color on the chromatic scale.

Example: Yellow + a little orange → "orangish-yellow";

Yellow + a little green → "greenish-yellow."

In this way one obtains warm or cold shades (fig. 71).

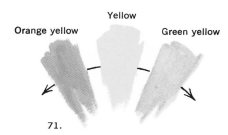

Yellow

Orange yellow                                    Green yellow

71.

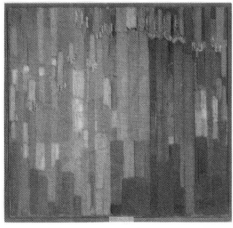

72. Arrangement of vertical yellows. Kupka (Museum of Modern Art, Paris).

73. Shades of green. Saint Jerome in the Desert (detail). Patenier (Louvre).

Color Scale

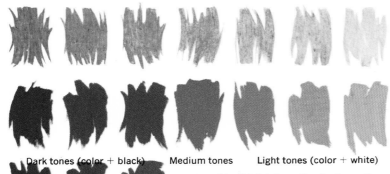

Dark tones (color + black)    Medium tones    Light tones (color + white)

74. Paint taken directly from the tube is, in the scale of values, more or less close to either white or black. For red, however, the paint usually corresponds to a medium tone.

Color + complement

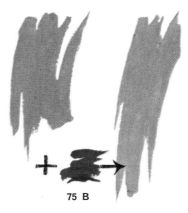

75 A                              75 B

A. Mixed color                    B. Colored gray

To "tone down" a color is to diminish its intensity, its brilliance.
To "heighten" a color is to make it more vivid, more intense.

# TONES — TINTED GRAYS MIXED COLORS

## I — TONES, SCALES

- **Tones** of a color are the different degrees of value of that color.

    Light tones are obtained by adding white.

    Dark tones are obtained by adding black.

- The **scale** is the range of tones in a color.

    Example: Red scale (fig. 74):
    Red + 3 whites
    Red + 2 whites
    Red + 1 white
    Pure red
    Red + 1 black
    Red + 2 blacks
    Red + 3 blacks

    (1 black = a small quantity of black; 2 blacks = slightly more black, etc.)

- **Dark tones** in a color may also be obtained by adding its complementary color (fig. 74).

## II — TINTED GRAYS, TONED-DOWN COLORS

- The mixture of a large quantity of gray + a small quantity of a color gives a *colored gray* (fig. 75).

    A toned-down color can be obtained by adding:

    — either a little gray (black + white)

    — or a little of its complement (which dulls it).

# OBSERVATION OF COLORS

To distinguish red from blue is simple; to recognize the quality of a given red is less simple and to reproduce it on a sheet of white paper requires experience and a good method of observation.

Let us take, for example, a sheet of red drawing paper, and try to reproduce the red as nearly as possible. Vermilion may appear to be the basic color, but if one dabs white paper with vermilion as it comes from the tube, it appears darker and more orange. By adding a little white and carmine the difference is noticeably less and the result obtained after drying is not far from the original: the tone, the shade and brilliance of the two colors are almost the same.

Thus, we now know to what colored mixture the red corresponds and yet *many factors can modify its appearance*. To observe this, let us cut from the same red paper three equal squares, numbered to facilitate the experiment, and also a much smaller circle (the size of confetti). We shall use squares 1 and 2 for the experimentation and square 3 as a point of comparison.

77

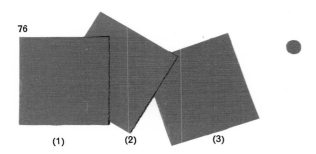

76

(1)　　　(2)　　　(3)

## EXPERIMENTS

- Place: square 1 on a sheet of black paper;

    square 2 on a sheet of white paper;

    and compare them.

The red surface of square 1 appears lighter, while the red surface of square 2 appears darker. Now the red has not changed, as a comparison with square 3 will prove. There is a modification of value, but it is only an *apparent* one (fig. 77).

78

- Put square 1 on a sheet of white paper and farther away on the same paper the circle of the same color. We note that the latter seems darker although it was cut from the same paper (fig. 78).

**Thus, the tone of a color depends on adjoining values and on its own surface area.**

- Now let us place square 1 on a green background and square 2 on an orange background. Square 1 appears much more brilliant than square 2 because it has been placed on its complementary color, green (see also p. 36).

These experiments have been made indoors in an even light. However, if this light changes, the quality of the red will be modified.

If a ray of light is projected on part of a sheet of red paper, the red in this spot becomes brighter, more orange and brilliant.

Conversely, the same red in the shade appears darker, more purplish and duller; and in the dark it is no different from black.

**These modifications of color due to lighting** can also be verified in the following way: fold the sheet of paper in two and hold it vertically in front of a spotlight in such a way that only half the paper receives the direct light. The red is darker and duller in the shade, clear and brilliant in the lighted part.

The experiment can also be made in a slightly different manner: roll the paper into a cylindrical form and hold it vertically in front of the lamp. The same variations of red are found, but this time the passage from the light tone to the dark is composed of half-tones (or a graded tone).

The same observations can, of course, be made by replacing lamplight by daylight: the folded or rolled paper is simply held up to the window.

## CONCLUSION

**The notion of color is relative:** for a given surface it depends on:

— Adjoining values;

— The colors surrounding it;

— The lighting.

It can also be shown that texture plays a role in the apparent quality of a color. By spreading an even coat of red gouache on a smooth piece of Bristol board, on a highly grained matte paper, and on a piece of white

percale we see that the differences in texture of these three backings are such that the red seems to change from one surface to the next.

79. The red legs of the person on the left, against a dark background, seem lighter than the red legs of the person on the right, seen on a gray background. Italian Primitive (Museum of Decorative Arts, Paris).

80. The red of this cloth is not the same in the shadowy folds as in the lighted parts of the cylindrical folds. The Lictors Bring Brutus the Bodies of his Sons (detail). David (Louvre).

40

81. Architecture. Piero della Francesca (Ducal Palaces, Urbino).

# BASIC ASPECTS OF PERSPECTIVE

## INTRODUCTION

### DEFINITION

The purpose of the observation drawing is to represent the subjects observed (objects, people, structures, landscapes, etc.) such as the spectator sees them from a particular place.

### HISTORY

In all ages man has tried, for many reasons, to depict objects, animals, landscapes as accurately as possible.

It was during the Renaissance in Europe, in the fifteenth and sixteenth centuries, that the sciences of nature and man were developed. Drawing then became a method of study. The greatest minds of the time applied themselves to discovering the laws by which they could better observe and depict the world around them.

Painters, architects, scholars wrote valuable books on the subject; they even invented instruments for the verification of those laws which, taken as a whole, form the subject of perspective.

In order to draw more accurately "in perspective," inventors found a method of producing on a plane surface the image of the outside world.

It was called the *camera oscura*, "the dark room," ancestor of the modern "camera." One could reproduce the image thus obtained by outlining it with a pencil; thus the painter copied directly the object he wanted to depict.

By piercing a small hole in the wall of a dark room

41

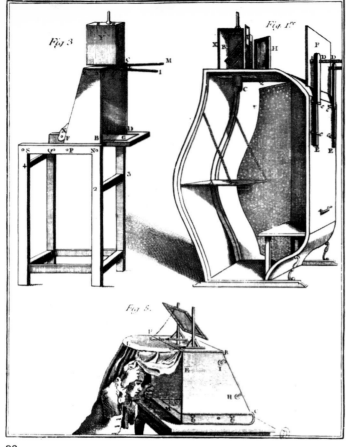

82.

one can project the image of outside objects on a screen placed in front of the hole; the images are reversed, colored, and all the more distinct because much more brightly lighted (fig. 82).

83. The painter at work, taken from "La perspective pratique." Père Jean Dubrevil, 1624.

"You choose a stationary object, a tree for example, and in front of a windowpane, with your eyes remaining in the same position and at the same level, you draw on the pane, following the contours of the tree which you have before your eyes; then move backwards until the real tree appears to be the same size as the one you have drawn; after this, paint your drawing to resemble in color and form the real tree so that, by closing an eye, both appear the same in color and equidistant from your eye."
Leonardo da Vinci.

# PERSPECTIVE AND OBSERVATION (I)

Photography is now a quick and convenient means of capturing the image of objects the memory of which we want to conserve.

Here are two photographs: they represent a plate and an automobile wheel, both circular objects (figs. 84 and 85). However, these photographs *do not show us circles* but curved, flattened forms, one horizontal, the other vertical. Yet we recognize a wheel and a plate, not only because of the details which permit us to identify them, but also because we are accustomed to these deformations.

84

85

86 ▶

Now let us look at this photograph of a cylindrical bird cage (fig. 86):

— Circle 1 is seen from above;

— Circle 2 is seen at camera level;

— Circle 3 is seen from below.

Notice that in one instance (circle 2) a circle appears to be a straight line.

43

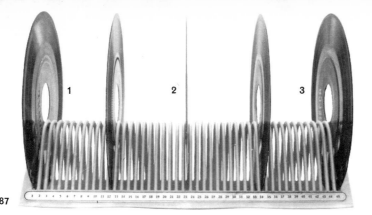

87

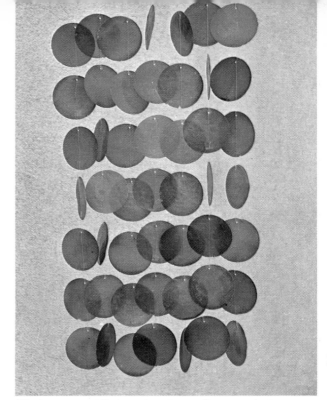

88. Japanese mobile in mother-of-pearl. (Janie Pradier.)

89

Now let's look at the photograph above:

— Record 1 is to the left of the camera;

— Record 2 is directly in front of the camera;

— Record 3 is to the right of the camera.

Notice that in this case, too, record 2 appears to us as a straight line.

**In all other positions the circle appears to be more or less flattened.** Mathematicians teach us that its apparent form is that of an **ellipse.**

An ellipse is a regular, closed curve in which there is no circle arc; it has two axes of symmetry. Here are several ellipses (fig. 88) (see also p. 61).

Finally, look at this photograph of a cylinder seen straight-on from the end (fig. 89). The circle in front and the circle at the other end both appear as circles, but the more distant one appears smaller.

**1.** We see a circle as a circle when it is perpendicular to our line of vision.

**2.** It appears proportionately smaller with distance.

**CONCLUSION**

**A.** The apparent form of an object depends on:

   **1)** its position with regard to our line of vision;

   **2)** its distance from us.

**B.** A circle is most often seen as an ellipse.

44

# PERSPECTIVE AND OBSERVATION (II)

By looking at this photograph (fig. 90) we can verify the conclusions of the preceding discussion. We notice in particular that the most distant pillars appear smaller to us than the others. Their dimension, height and width seem to diminish with distance.

So, knowing that the more distant an object is, the smaller it appears to us, we can study the different views of the same cube (fig. 91).

We see that the farther side of the cube seems smaller than the one nearer to us. The lateral surfaces which connect them are thus deformed.

Note that when a side of a cube is seen straight-on, it is because it lies precisely along our line of vision. It appears to us as a straight line.

If the cube is just opposite the observer the apparent diminution of the more distant surface is evident.

Now let's look at figure 92. While the intersections facing us seem to diminish with distance, the perpendicular intersections which join them seem to draw closer together with distance. Only the intersections that face us appear vertical or horizontal. Parallel straight lines receding from us thus appear to converge with distance.

Study the various views of the cube and note the deformations of the faces and intersections:

**1.** A square has the form of a square when it is perpendicular to our line of vision;

**2.** The farther away from us it is, the smaller it appears;

**3.** Parallel straight lines appear to converge with distance.

90. Look at the distances between the posts. Look at the height of the portico. What do you notice?

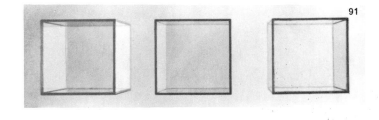

## CONCLUSION

**A.** The apparent form of an object depends on its position in relation to our line of vision and on its distance.

**B.** Parallel straight lines appear to converge as they recede.

93. Duck
Florilège de
Nassau Idstein.
Hans Hang
(Museum of
Strasbourg).

94    Note: In the same way, for a profile portrait, a photographer will leave a
wider margin in front of the face (the more complicated contour).

# BASIC ASPECTS OF OBSERVATION DRAWING

## PAGE LAYOUT

To compose a drawing is to place it on the sheet of paper in a carefully planned **dimension** and in the best **location.**

The drawing should be surrounded by a more or less wide, empty margin to set it off. Thus we must:

**1.** Define the relationship between "full" and "blank" space or, in other terms, determine the dimensions of the drawing according to the dimensions of the page:

— Too small a drawing appears lost on the page;

— Too large a drawing appears to be squeezed in.

**2.** Distribute the blank space in relation to the full, that is, locate the subject in the correct position.

There are two situations:

a) **The subject to be depicted is symmetrical.**

Example: a butterfly with outspread wings (see p. 72).

In this case, the vertical median line of the sheet of paper should coincide with the axis of symmetry of the butterfly.

To avoid too central a setting, which is uninteresting, place the butterfly slightly above or below the center to create unequal margins.

b) **The subject to be depicted is not symmetrical.**

Example: a branch.

It should be arranged on the paper in such a way that the empty space corresponding to the most complicated side of the branch is greater than that on the simpler side (fig. 94).

95. Pictographic signs.

# THE OBSERVATION DRAWING DRAFT AND CHARACTER

It is the mind that hears and sees.
Montaigne

DRAWING, in its most general meaning, is the art of depicting by means of lines and shadows the forms of beings and objects, real or imaginary.

**A drawing from nature is not a simple mechanical imitation of what is set before our eyes;** it is necessary to study an object first in order to understand it. In this way, the object, however complicated, will be easier to draw.

## DRAFT AND CHARACTER

**1.** The **rough draft** should materialize the mind's work.

The rough draft is a simplified or diagrammatic form intended to demonstrate or help comprehension. It is, in a way, a "drawn résumé." It expresses the general structure of an object and assists in the comprehension of its construction, volume, and form.

47

96. Various figures. Album Saint-Germain. Villard de Honnecourt (Bibliothèque Nationale, Paris).

A few examples:

The draft of an acacia leaflet (robinia) (fig. 97) can be made by sketching an oval curve, the draft of the leaf itself being composed of a number of smaller ovals.

The draft of a clover leaf is made with three equal ovals (fig. 98).

For a pair of glasses seen from the front, two ovals placed side by side would be used (fig. 99).

The draft of a pair of scissors will indicate their form and whether they are open or closed (fig. 100).

Objects having the same function or the same use often have the same structure, thus the same draft.

Keys, for example, can all be drafted in the same manner even if the handles vary in roundness and detail, the stems are more or less long and decorated with collars, the bits more or less large or cut out (fig. 101).

Volumes, too, can be expressed by rough drafts.

This one (fig. 102) describes an open umbrella as well as a mushroom.

The other (fig. 103) indicates a roof as well as a tent.

We should remember, then, that any object, any creature, in movement or not, can be represented by *a draft plan which expresses its structure.*

In a manner of speaking, this draft constitutes the bond between the function and the form; it is an indispensable element in the elaboration of the drawing.

**2.** After the analysis of the general structure our attention will be given to *characterizing* what we want to represent.

The "character" is, above all, the distinctive mark of objects or beings, the particularities which distinguish them from other objects or beings: their individual proportions, positions, forms, colors, substances.

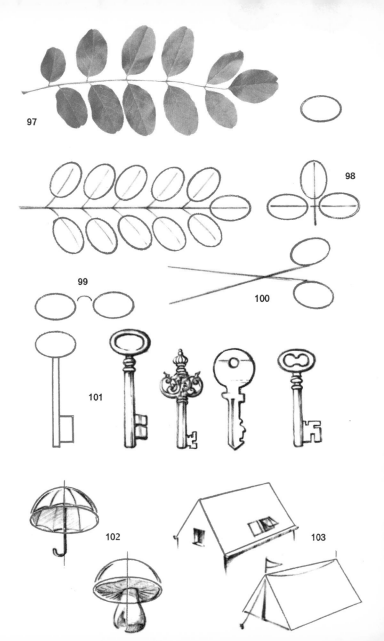

One can easily discern the character of an object by comparing it to another object of the same nature but of different proportions. The contrast will affirm the particular character of each of them.

In drawing, then, one must "bring out" and accentuate the dominant character of the model.

105. In this bird, everything appears sharp, lively, pointed. Bird. Bernard Buffet.

104. Contrast in proportions: heavy body, thick feet, small head. Bird. Pisanello (Louvre).

106. The massiveness of the body and the two deep, strange eyes express the dominant characteristics of a bird of prey at rest. Eagle owl. Pompon.

**49**

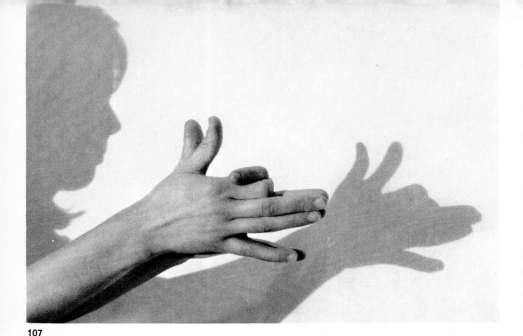

107

# DIRECTIONS AND PROPORTIONS

We have all made "shadow pictures" (fig. 107). The animals, people, or subjects portrayed did not need inner details to be expressive and alive. The positions and proportions were all the essentials needed to give the forms their meaning and character.

## NOTIONS OF DIRECTIONS AND PROPORTIONS

**1.** Directions (fig. 108):

Let's observe this runner seen in profile, first kneeling at the starting line, then ready to go and finally in full action. It is the same person in all the pictures: he has the same build, his arms and legs are always the same in dimension; only the DIRECTIONS or positions of the head, the trunk and limbs change and characterize the different stages of motion.

108

50

Here are two pairs of scissors (fig. 109): the first is open, the second closed. The lengths, widths and shapes are identical; only the DIRECTIONS (or positions) of the blades are different. To draw them one must first carefully observe the *angle* formed by the *directions* of the blades.

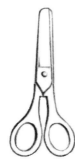

109

110. The varying directions of trunks and limbs suggest movement. Runners on a Grecian vase (Vatican).

111. The diversified directions here reveal a subtle equilibrium. Mobile by Calder (Maeght Gallery, Paris).

112. Don Quixote and Sancho Panza. Daumier.

113. Don Quixote and Sancho Panza. Picasso. Like Daumier, Picasso has used to a maximum the contrast in proportions between Cervantes' two characters.

## 2. Proportions:

In drawings of the long and lanky Don Quixote perched on the scrawny Rosinante and followed by the fat, solid Sancho Panza squashed on his donkey, it is the comic element in the contrast of PROPORTIONS which has often tempted the artist (figs. 112, 113).

These two bottles placed side by side have the same height and the same width. Their general dimensions are the same; that is, their height and largest width are identical. Yet they do not resemble each other (fig. 114). This contrast is essentially due to their differences in PROPORTION.

115. These vases are composed of the same elements (body, neck, handles) but their proportions are different. After Zurbaran, Vases (Prado, Madrid).

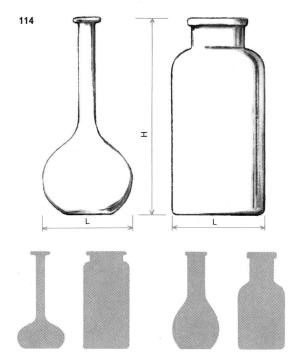

114

The first has a long neck and narrow opening, like the stork in the fable, while the second has a wide, flat neck and a voluminous body which occupies most of its height.

If, in drawing these bottles, one did not take all their proportions into consideration, the result would be freakish.

In conclusion we can say that DIRECTIONS and PROPORTIONS constitute the two basic elements in observation drawing.

53

## OBSERVATION OF DIRECTIONS AND PROPORTIONS

**1. Directions:**

Whether in nature or among the objects which surround us, HORIZONTAL and VERTICAL directions or positions are common and rather easy to find: the walls of most buildings reproduce the vertical position verified by the mason's plumb line (fig. 116).

The horizon line on the sea, seen over a very short distance, is the very image of the horizontal direction. The mason's spirit level is an instrument which verifies horizontal directions.

**All other directions are said to be oblique.**

The student should train his eye to see horizontal and vertical directions.

— The vertical lines of all the objects that we shall draw can be verified with the aid of a plumb line, an instrument which is easy to make (fig. 116).

With a little practice a crayon or ruler can easily be held correctly in a vertical position to serve as a means of comparison (fig. 117).

• On the other hand, it is scarcely possible to use a spirit level to verify the horizontal direction we wish to draw, so it becomes necessary to practice sighting it correctly by holding a pencil horizontally at arm's length (fig. 118).

• In drawing, vertical directions are represented by straight lines parallel to the right and left sides of the page, and horizontal directions by straight lines parallel to the upper and lower edges of the page.

We can determine other directions by evaluating the angles formed with the horizontal or vertical directions

117

116

118

119

120

121. Tile. Baptistry of Florence.

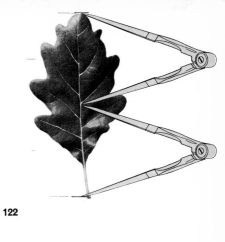

122

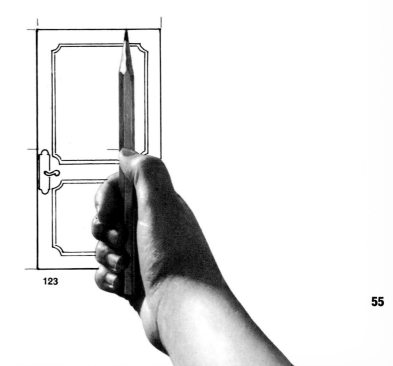

123

or with other oblique directions already drawn (fig. 119).

**2.** Proportions:

Simple proportions or those concerning known forms are easily estimated by eye (figs. 120, 121).

In most cases, proportions are evaluated by comparing SIZES.

The width of this oak leaf (fig. 122) is equal to half its length. We can also say that its width can be contained twice in its length, or that its length is double its width.

When we want to note the proportions of a rather large object, or one beyond our reach, the comparison of proportions can be made at a distance.

Thus without knowing the exact sizes, we can nevertheless say that the height of this door is twice its width (fig. 123).

55

124

## SILHOUETTES AND SURFACES

A folded paper like the one above presents a number of different angles and directions. Placed against the light in front of a window it reveals only its silhouette, which, however, is enough to show the general character of its form.

125

This obliges us not only to evaluate proportions and directions but to observe surfaces or shapes. The empty areas around the contour of this silhouette are also very important (fig. 125). An appreciation of their shapes will help us to draw the silhouette of the model.

Thus, we should bear in mind that, because of its emphasis on empty and full spaces, the silhouette completes, defines and individualizes the draft of any object.

126. Various vases    photographed with back-lighting.

### USE OF DIRECTIONS AND PROPORTIONS IN THE LAYOUT OF A FREEHAND DRAWING

The map of France presents complicated contours. If we wanted to reproduce it, and weren't fussy about the size, we could simply trace it from the nearest atlas. However, to draw France to a different scale, we need another approach. Let us proceed methodically.

First, observe the proportions of the country: the largest width, at the Brittany level (Ouessant), is equal to its greatest height, from Dunkirk to the frontier of the eastern Pyrénées (Port-Vendres) (fig. 127).

Thus, the whole map can be drawn in a square. We'll begin our drawing with a light outline (or sketch) of that geometric form.

• Between pins stuck in the map we'll stretch a piece of string which *envelops* all the contours (fig. 128). The polygon formed in this way is an irregular hexagon (its sides are not entirely equal). Observe the location of its points: some are situated on the outline of the enveloping square, some are near it.

On the drawing place Dunkirk on the upper edge of the square, slightly to the right of center.

We see, with the aid of our pencil held vertically, that the vertical straight line beginning at this city also passes through Paris, situated approximately at the upper fourth of the vertical line.

The horizontal line passing through Paris approximately joins the farthest points in the east and west: the Island of Ouessant and the Rhine.

The lines from Dunkirk to Ouessant and to the Rhine can thus be sketched in.

**127**

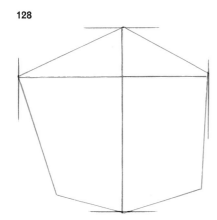

**128**

A string stretched across the map helps us to see these directions; our pencil held at arm's length serves the same purpose. By prolonging these oblique directions, by comparing them to the horizontal or vertical directions which we have already traced, we can estimate and verify their exact positions. Working in the same way we can place on our square Bayonne, Port-Vendres and Nice, and we can trace, after verifying their directions, the other sides of the hexagon outlining the map of France.

We can now continue our drawing by trying to approximate the irregularities of the contours. By continuing to estimate proportions we can place on the hexagonal outline such salient points as Cap Gris-Nez, north of Boulogne, and Cap de la Hague, near Cherbourg.

Similar observations permit us to make a rough sketch of the coastline itself between the two capes, and between Cap de la Hague and Ouessant in Brittany.

We can now mark the silhouette of the hollowed-out forms such as that on the Atlantic coast from Ouessant to Hendaye, south of Bayonne, passing through Quiberon, the Island of Ré and Arcachon, points which are easy to recognize in relation to the side of the hexagon Ouessant-Bayonne.

The Mediterranean coast, the broad outline of the frontiers of the north, the east and south can be sketched in the same way.

Having reached this point, we can say that our drawing of France is *in position*.

This positioning gives us only the silhouette of France: the interior details have not yet been begun, nor have the precise details of the contours been filled in, but the general picture is already a good likeness (fig. 130).

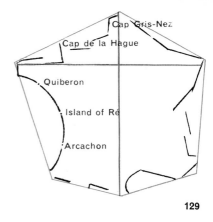

**129**

**130**

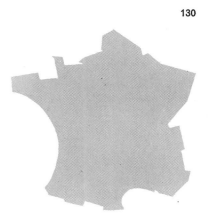

**57**

- **Application:** the positioning of a plane-tree leaf, drawn full-size.

The method of drawing a leaf would be the same.

The light paper on which we have placed it brings out the richness of the colors and makes its silhouette perfectly distinct (fig. 131).

After observing its over-all proportions — the width in comparison with the length — we have drawn the direction of its principal rib, lengthened by the stem, and sketched the enveloping form. To the different points of this enveloping polygon we have drawn the lateral ribs, their tips having been determined and their directions verified.

These lines already indicate a certain number of shapes which must be compared to the corresponding shapes of the model (fig. 132).

By referring to the elements already in place — the tips and the ribs — let us try to determine the directions of the sides of the most deeply cut-out areas (fig. 133).

To observe the angles more easily, we have extended the sides to find the points where they meet the established outer guide lines.

Thus, we can control the shapes of the blank spaces formed by the contours of the leaf and the enveloping polygon.

So far we have only carried out the positioning of the leaf, but already the contours are visible, the hollow and projecting parts are carved out (like the gulfs, bays, and capes on the profile of the map of France).

We must now study the shapes of the contours and the interior elements.

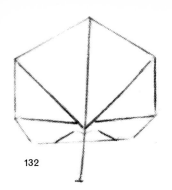

132

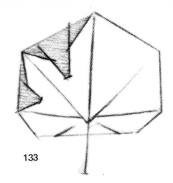

133

## REMARKS CONCERNING
## THE "ENVELOPING FORM"

**1.** If, instead of a plane-tree leaf, we choose a nasturtium or geranium leaf, the enveloping form will be a circle (fig. 134).

A clover leaf will be inscribed in a triangle, a bay leaf between two arcs (fig. 135).

Thus, the enveloping form is not necessarily composed of straight line segments, nor is it necessarily formed by continuous lines.

**2.** Draft and enveloping form: the enveloping form is not the draft and cannot be substituted for it; both are indispensable in drawing, one does not replace the other.

Thus all clover leaves can be represented in a draft by three ovals (fig. 136), while the clover leaf we have chosen is inscribed in a triangular enveloping form which is appropriate to it.

**The draft corresponds to the "thought-out" part of the drawing** while the **enveloping form corresponds to the "observed" part.**

The draft sums up "the general idea" of the model; the enveloping form is a very simplified representation, but nonetheless one which is already individualized.

134 A

134 B

135

136 A

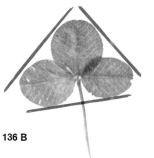

136 B

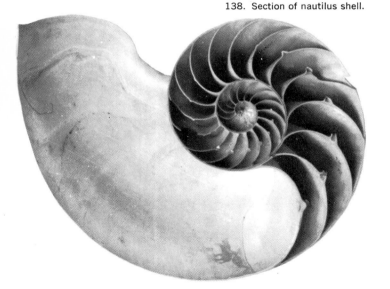

137. Quartz crystal.

138. Section of nautilus shell.

In the various examples we have used in our study of directions and proportions we have not extended our work beyond positioning, or layout.

The representation of the model is still in a very simplified state: we have been mainly concerned with indicating contours in their **general outline.**

A precise and thorough study of FORMS, exterior as well as interior, now becomes an important step.

Forms contribute greatly to **personalizing** the subject that we want to draw.

## THE NATURE OF FORMS

Form is essentially a question of the configuration of objects — their appearance — and concerns lines as well as surface-areas.

Forms are of two types:

— Forms composed of straight lines (fig. 137);

— Forms composed of curved lines (fig. 138).

Nature offers us an infinite variety of curved forms. On the other hand, straight forms are for the most part due to the work of man. One frequently finds in the world of forms combinations of straight and curved lines.

• **A straight line** is defined geometrically as the shortest distance between two points. We understand this implicitly when we draw one.

We can "materialize" a straight line in a taut string: the plumb line is a specific example.

It should be noted that we can observe and draw only fragments of straight lines; in geometry these are called **segments** of straight lines.

Such segments placed end to end in different directions form a broken line.

- **The curved line:**

There are a great many different kinds of curves.

We are already acquainted with the circle. The aspect of an arc of a circle depends not only on its length but also on the radius of the circle.

Some curves are formed by fragments of circles joined together — ovals, ovoids, undulations, spirals — and can be drawn with a compass (fig. 139).

We shall have occasion to observe and draw many other curved lines which are not formed by fragments of circles.

The ellipse (fig. 140) discussed in another chapter can be more or less flat. It should be drawn freehand.

The variety of non-circular curves is so great that in industrial design an instrument called the "French curve" is used. It presents the most widely varied profiles of curves (fig. 141).

The evenness of an outline made with a drawing-pen sometimes requires the use of a flexible device with which curves can be shaped by hand according to the form to be drawn.

**The curved line is a rich and living form.**

With the curved line the artist comes closer to animated nature; the work is less rigid and cold, for the curve possesses warmth and life.

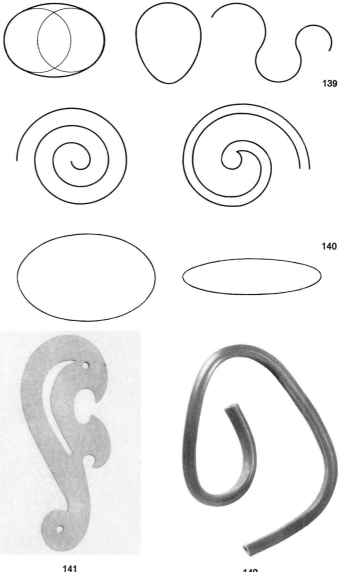

139

140

141

142

143. This pillar in the Church of the Jacobins in Toulouse is called "the palm tree."

144. In the helicoidal form of this tower. Gaudi affirms his liking for supple shapes from which the straight line is excluded. Guëll Chapel, 1914 (Barcelona).

145. These chairs by Eero Saarinen (Knoll International, France) are reminiscent of shells or some ample floral forms.

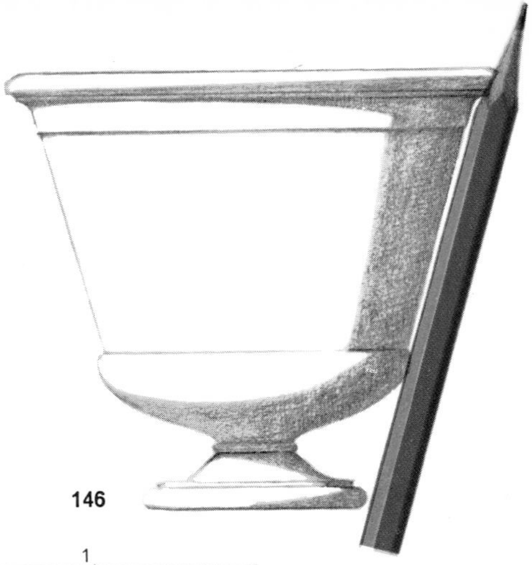

**146**

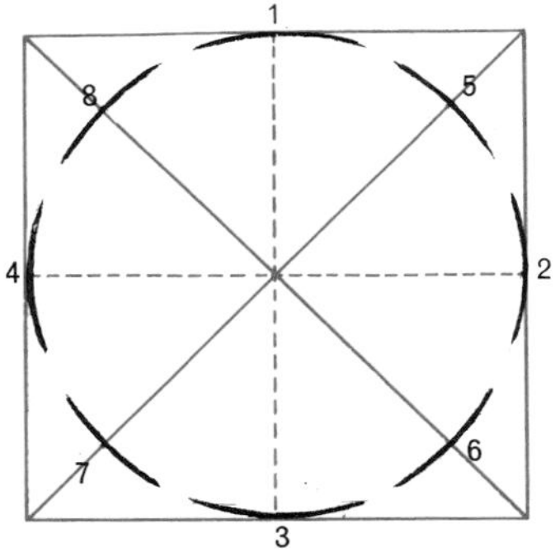

**147**

**148**

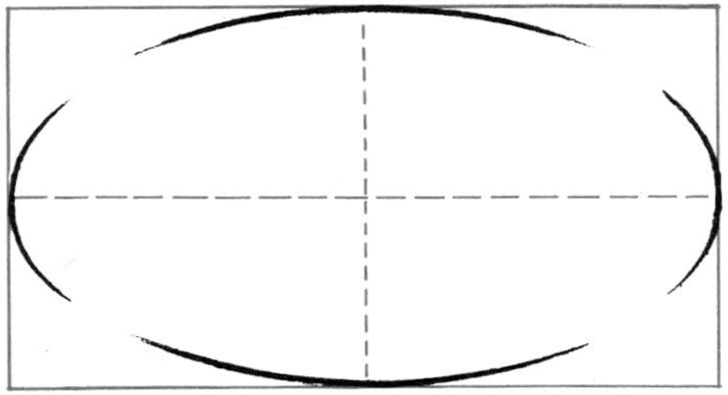

## OBSERVATION AND REPRESENTATION OF FORMS

### • Forms composed of straight lines:

It is fairly simple to see what form or fragment of a form should be depicted by a straight line: we can hold our pencil tilted in the same direction (fig. 146).

To draw this straight line it is sufficient to determine its direction, and evaluate its length in the drawing.

### • Forms composed of curved lines:

The analysis of a curved line is more subtle.

It should first be stated that even in the rather rare case where we are called upon to draw a perfect circle, it should be drawn freehand. It would be out of place to employ a compass in an observation drawing. Thus, we will never have to find the precise center of a curved line; rather, several observations and notations will lead us progressively to a definite outline.

In drawing a circle freehand, we make use of some of its geometric characteristics. Let's study a circle inscribed in a square. It is tangent to the square at four points (1, 2, 3, 4). Four other points (5, 6, 7, 8) are situated on the diagonals. Let us mark on the sides of the square and on the diagonals those eight points of the circle (fig. 147). On joining them evenly by small sections of curves we achieve a very satisfactory sketch of a circle.

The ellipse is related to the circle, but is symmetrical around two axes instead of one. Thus, two different sets of curves have to be sketched (fig. 148). The same procedure is used as for the circle.

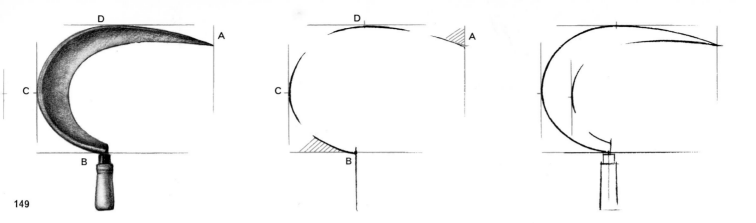

149

— The flattened and open curve of a sickle (fig. 149) resembles none of the geometric curved lines that we know.

Observe the outside edge of the blade. Its curve can be inscribed in a rectangle which passes through point A as well as through the part attached to the handle at B. The upper side touches the curve at only one point, D, the left side at C. In geometry it is said that these sides are "tangent" to the curve at points C and D.

These observations will help us in laying out the drawing. Once the proportions of the rectangle are noted and the rectangle is sketched, we can mark on its sides first the points A and B, the limits of the curve, then the positions of points C and D, where the curve is tangent to the sides of the rectangle. It will be noted that the curve is very flat in the upper part while the arc at the left is more curved.

Sketch in lightly these two different curves at points

C and D. Observe the angle the curve at A makes with the right side of the rectangle, and at B with the lower edge of the rectangle. We can now determine the direction of the curve: from point A toward point D and from point B toward point C.

Similar observations concerning the angles between C and D and the rectangle will allow us to determine precisely the directions of the curve at these points.

The outer edge of the sickle is now indicated by four fragments to be joined together.

The same type of observations will help us to sketch the inner edge. It can be drawn fairly easily if the variations in the width of the blade are evaluated.

As a general rule, we can find a base for drawing curved lines, however complicated they may be, by beginning with a polygon or polygonal form — that is, with segments of straight lines whose directions we can determine.

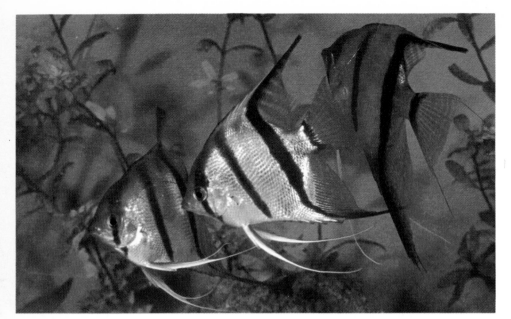

150. Tropical fish with graceful, delicate curves, in an aquarium.

## EXPRESSION OF FORMS

**The contour of a form is expressed by a line.** This line is straight or curved according to the profile of the form.

In a preceding chapter dealing with the technique of the line, advice was given on the procedure, the characteristics to look for, and the possibilities offered.

To sketch a straight line one can either make a single stroke in the desired direction or proceed by shorter segments joined together.

In sketching or drawing a curved line, the hand should remain as much as possible in the center of the curve, that is, in the concavity of the curve. A back-and-forth movement of the hand, with the wrist, the elbow, or even the shoulder serving as the center, allows the pencil to sketch a fairly large curve.

**Surfaces** will, for the most part, be treated in terms of light and dark tones (see p. 15) which will express reliefs and hollows.

# THE DOCUMENTARY STUDY

151. After a manuscript border. Book of Hours, 15th century.

## DEFINITION

A "documentary" or "realistic" study is an exercise which consists of representing *with exactitude* an object or a natural element. This "document" or representation should give us precise details about the form and value, the color and substance of the object or element.

## USES

**The documentary study can be:**

— **A document created to be looked at** in the same way as a landscape, a portrait or a composition (fig. 155);

— **A document for study:** the archeologist, the naturalist or the surgeon can analyze it and draw conclusions from it as he would from the original;

— **A document to interpret:** it can give a decorator inspiration for forms, colors and the effects of materials (fig. 154);

— **An advertising document:** The commercial artist who does illustrations intended to launch a new product sometimes creates a documentary study far more expressive than a photograph.

152. Still life. Oudry (Museum of Fine Arts, Marseilles).

67

153. Remains of a meal on the dining-room floor. Roman mosaic (Lateran Museum, Rome).

## PROBLEMS RAISED BY THE DOCUMENTARY STUDY

Assume that the subject has been selected, and that it is an isolated object.

**1.** Presentation of the subject.

Its most **picturesque aspect** should be chosen; its placement and lighting should bring out its character clearly. Experiment by placing the subject on white paper if the study is to be made on white paper.

**2.** Choice of the scale of representation.

It is difficult to draw a model larger than life; it is wiser at first to reproduce it in its **true dimensions** or to **reduce** it slightly, depending on its actual size.

**3.** Composition (see p. 46):

By a careful distribution of used and unused space one can achieve a **balanced** placement adapted to the form of the model and the dimensions of the sheet of paper.

**4.** Execution:

a) Construction (see p. 70):

A light sketch of the general form is made, proportions being carefully respected; errors are corrected and contours made more precise; then the areas of shade and light are indicated, and finally the essential details are added.

b) Choice of technique:

**This choice is guided by the subject:** each technique presents advantages and disadvantages. Gouache is indispensable for expressing the velvet texture of a butter-fly or the iridescent pearly luster of seashells. Watercolor is more suitable to the transparency of many flowers.

The fine-pointed brush permits a compact, precise execution; a stiff brush is good for rendering downy or rough substances (lichen, moss, tree bark).

Finally, the pencil, the simplest instrument, is appropriate whenever the colors and substances do not require the use of paint.

154. 18th-century silk (Historical Museum of Textiles, Lyon).

155. Documentary and decorative study of flowers. Giralomo Rini (Museum of Decorativ Arts, Paris).

**68**

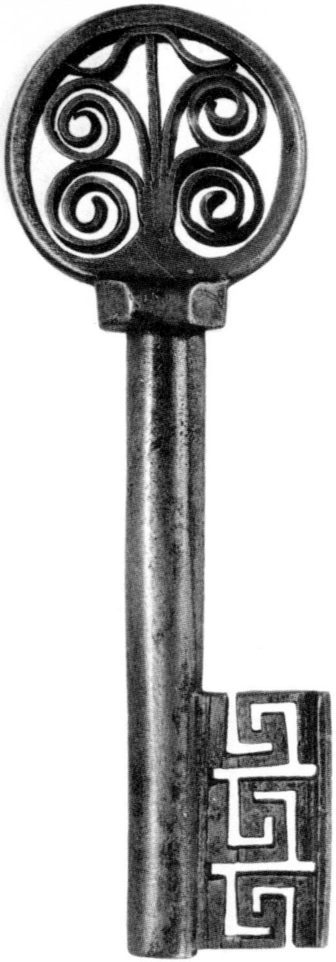

156. Key (Le Secq des Tournelles Museum, Rouen).

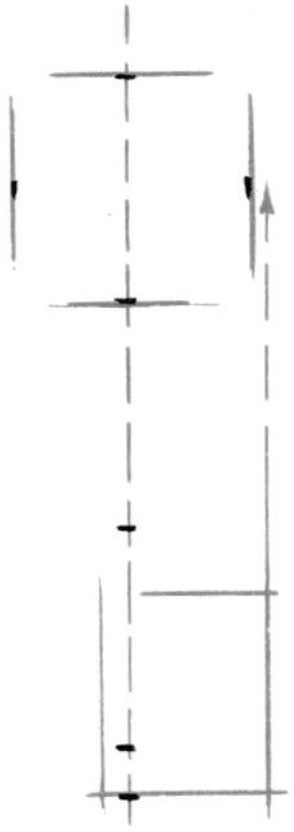

157. A

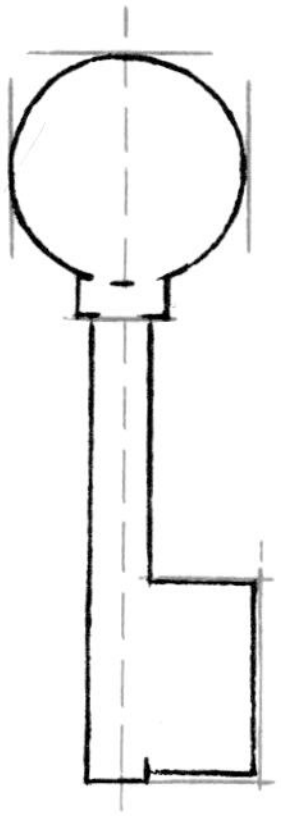

157. B

# EXAMPLES OF FREEHAND DRAWING

### I. Analysis of geometric forms

A key (fig. 156).

Before drawing an object, whatever it may be, it is of the utmost importance to make a brief verbal analysis of it to uncover its general and special characteristics, and determine its sketch-plan.

Then we shall methodically follow the procedures we have discussed for placing it on the page and sketching its proportions and forms. Finally, the execution will permit us to express its volume, substance and, if need be, its color.

**1.** Analysis of the model:

The **plan** of this antique key is divided into three parts: the handle, the stem, and the "bit" which turns the lock.

The handle of the key is decorated with two superimposed sets of spirals on each side of the axis.

A rather thick polygonal collar joins it to the **stem.** which is a thick cylinder.

The cut-outs on the bit, necessary to the mechanism, here form a "Greek" decoration.

**2.** Placement (see p. 46):

The form and size of a piece of drawing paper suggest a vertical representation of the key.

The general direction given by the axis of the stem will be indicated by a vertical line.

**3.** Proportions (fig. 157):

Once the key's axis has been sketched, we can decide on the total length of our drawing. This, in turn, will determine all the other proportions.

In the present case it is not necessary to draw the whole enveloping rectangle, but simply the two extreme elements, the handle and the bit, evaluating their different proportions.

Since the handle is circular (its width is equal to its height), it can be inscribed in a square.

The diameter of the circle, equal to a side of the square, is contained slightly more than three times in the height of the key.

Note the level of the bit with regard to the handle. Now evaluate its width, which, including the stem, is about one-fifth the total height of the key. The height of the bit can be contained about three and two-thirds times in the total height.

Finally, let's evaluate visually the thickness of the stem and then verify it by comparison with the dimensions already determined.

The two end elements of the key (handle and bit) are thus placed on the axis in relation to each other and their proportions have been calculated by comparison with the whole.

**4.** Forms:

We can now draw the forms of the **general silhouette** before turning to the interior forms and decorations.

Sketch the circle of the handle, and the right and left sides of the stem.

By noting the height and width of the collar which joins the bow to the stem, the general sketch can be completed.

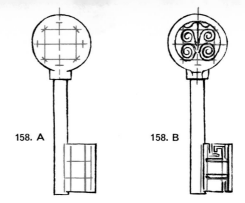

158. A    158. B

We can now place in position the interior elements and decorative forms. Using the drawings above, we can follow the different stages of the work (figs. 158 A and B).

**5.** Expression of volume and substance:

**The indication of substance** is closely related to that of volume in the representation of a metallic object.

Values can be indicated with a pencil. Apply a medium gray to the entire key, working more lightly on the shiny parts.

The darker parts (loop, collar, upper edge of the bit) should then be gone over again; some contours should be emphasized by a still darker or thicker line (see p. 32).

Spots and irregularities can be added afterwards.

By successive stages we have thus completed a faithful "portrait" of our subject.

159. Epiphora Bauhiniae, night butterfly (South Africa).

## II. Analysis of curved forms: a butterfly

Observations of the structure of a butterfly.

Three parts can be distinguished:

— The head, bent forward and almost invisible, has two feathery antennae;

— The thorax, rather short, to which are attached two pairs of flat, thin wings;

— The abdomen, formed of rings and ending in a point.

The bilateral symmetry of both the colored surfaces and the contours is one of its essential characteristics.

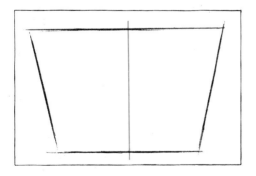

A

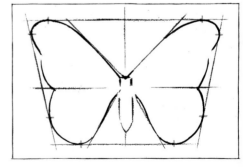

B

C

The butterfly will be drawn in life-size with its axis vertical.

The enveloping polygon is an isosceles trapezoid.

The sides of the trapezoid and a few well-chosen tangents limit the enveloping form of the wings.

The important points of the curves are also indicated.

Using these points the outline of the contours are drawn.

## Remarks on symmetry

a) Review of elementary notions:

— A figure possesses an axis of symmetry if the two sides coincide when folded along the axis;

— Two points symmetrical to the axis are situated on a straight line perpendicular to this axis and equidistant from it.

b) We can draw symmetrical elements more easily by sketching the two sides simultaneously.

We can check the symmetry by turning the page over and looking at the sketched forms through the paper, or by holding the drawing upside-down.

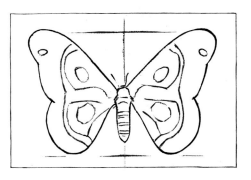

D

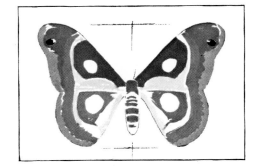

E

F

The silhouette of the colored areas is drawn in pencil.

A few details are indicated:
— Direction of the antennae;
— The rings on the abdomen.

The principal colored surfaces are first painted in flat tones.

The details can then be put in with light, delicate touches.

Avoid giving them too much importance.

## III. Analysis of irregular forms: the lower jaw of a rabbit

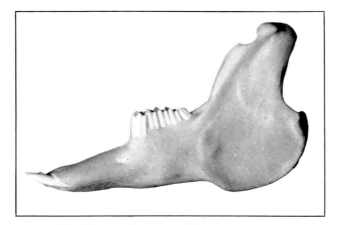

160. The natural sciences utilize drawings to note observations with precision.

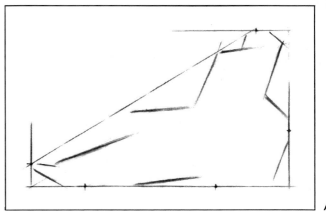

**A**

The drawing is laid in place by indicating the main proportions and the general directions.

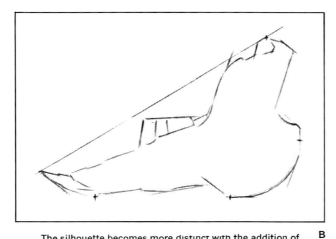

**B**

The silhouette becomes more distinct with the addition of important details: incisors, bar, molar and condyle.

The principal notches and curves are noted in their general outline.

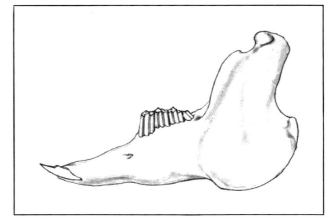

**C**

The important details are brought out by firm, clear strokes.

A light stroke accompanied by a very soft scumbling suggests the principal reliefs of the interior.

# IV. Analysis of simple volumes

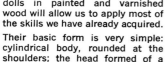

161. A portrait of these Japanese dolls in painted and varnished wood will allow us to apply most of the skills we have already acquired.

Their basic form is very simple: cylindrical body, rounded at the shoulders; the head formed of a somewhat flattened ball.

A

Detail of the head.
Carefully observe the direction and form of the ellipses of the father's hat.

B

Detail of the base.
The ellipses of the bases are very flat.

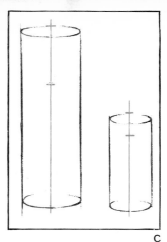

C

The enveloping cylinders indicate the positions and proportions of the two dolls.

For each figure the height of the head is evaluated in relation to the total height.

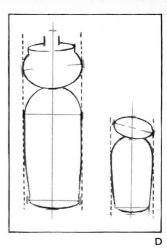

D

The different widths of the head, the chest and the base are noted at their respective levels.

The rounded contour of the shoulders is traced.

The color is roughed out in flat tone.

The local tone of light and shade already contributes to the suggestion of relief.

A few picturesque details are indicated. Highlights and reflections will help to render the substance.

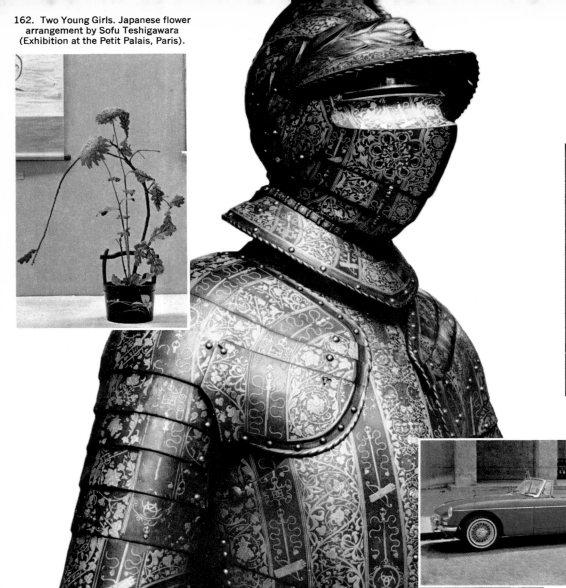

162. Two Young Girls. Japanese flower arrangement by Sofu Teshigawara (Exhibition at the Petit Palais, Paris).

164. Textile. Presentation in the Temple (detail). Master of the Holy Kinship. German school, 15th-16th centuries (Louvre).

165. Sports car.

163. The decoration adds nothing to the solidity of this armor . It is simple embellishment. Armor of Henry II (Army Museum, Pari

166. Fresco of Beni Hasan. Egypt,
XII dynasty, circa 1920-1900 B.C.

167. In this room substance and color are the "decoration."
Modern interior (La Maison Francaise).

# 3. DECORATION

168. Ceremonial brasero, terra cotta. Mexico. Aztec civilization 1324-1521 (Museum of Anthropology, Mexico).

169. Louis XV interior (Hotel Matignon).

# INTRODUCTION

# DECORATION

## I — INTRODUCTION

DECORATION is a need which has been felt in all countries, in all ages. Man decorates his dwelling, his possessions, his clothes (figs. 164, 167, 168, 169).

> "The instinct to decorate in man is as strong, or almost, as the need to eat; even the cave man experienced an overwhelming need to decorate, thus to ennoble" (Lurçat).

## II — DEFINITIONS

— The word "decoration" signifies, in a general sense: ornamentation, embellishment.

— "A decorative composition" is an arrangement of lines, areas, volumes, colors, textures, in a harmonious whole.

— The "decorative arts" are the arts applied to the decoration of common or luxury objects.

## III — CHARACTERISTICS

**1.** To decorate is to create; but to find subjects (motifs), to imagine arrangements, the decorator can derive in-

170. Sculpture inspired by the internal form of a seashell. Germaine Richier. The Spiral (Gallery Greuzevault, Paris).

171. Lantern. Star-shaped polyhedron. Spanish crafts.

172. Zoomorphic rhyton (drinking horn). End of 7th century B.C. (Museum of Archeology, Teheran).

173. Floral background. Tapestry. Late Gothic period (Museum of Cluny, Paris).

spiration from the most varied sources: nature, geometry, works of the past, etc. (figs. 170 to 174).

**2.** To decorate is to embellish a form:
— By respecting its character (fig. 175);
— By accentuating its character;
— By modifying its appearance.

**3.** To decorate is to call on all techniques:
— The clay arts: ceramics, faience, porcelain . . .;
— The glass arts: stained-glass, enamel, mosaics . . .;
— The metal arts: iron, bronze, precious metals . . .;
— The graphic arts: books, advertising . . .;
— The textile arts, the wood arts, the stone arts, etc.

174. A traditional design decorating a modern material: plastic imitation of tooled leather.

175. Lenticular bottle. Hittite art, 15th century B.C.

79

176. "Damascus" tile. Turkey, first half of 16th century (Museum of Decorative Arts, Paris).

177. Model of house built entirely of plastic.

178. Here, color plays a functional role (the yellow, for example corresponds to sulphurous gas.) Lacq, France.

179. "... There, that small vermilion dot ... a grain of salt ..." Paul Claudel.

In this picture the fisherman's red hat "heightens" the greens in the landscape. The Bridge of Nantes. Corot (Louvre).

# COLOR HARMONY

One may speak of the friendship or enmity of colors.   Poussin

Harmony is the basis of color theory. Baudelaire

**Color is one of the essential elements in decoration.** In all ages and among all peoples it has always played a large role. Today it is of great importance in every field (objects, clothing, furniture, architecture ...). Its use is often associated with metals and plastics (figs. 165, 177, and 178).

To make the best use of color it is thus necessary to have a good understanding of its laws.

## OBSERVATIONS

Certain colors go well together.

- **Because they are "analogous."**

Examples:

— One color, paler tones and darker tones of that color;

— One color and shades of it.

- **Or because they enhance each other by contrast.**

Examples:

— A warm color and a cold color;

— A light tone and a dark tone;

— A large quantity of one color and a small quantity of its complement.

Color harmony should thus include a balanced dosage of these analogies and contrasts.

180. Aubusson tapestry. Chantereine, by Jullien (La Demeure, Paris).

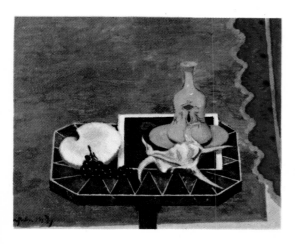

181. A subdued shade of the dominant color used on a large surface; a bright shade of the dominant on a smaller surface; an off-shade of its complement. Still life. Chapelain-Midi.

## METHOD FOR SEEKING COLOR HARMONY

While maintaining a basic unity, one should use a large variety of colors (figs. 180, 182):

- Choose a **dominant color;**
- Add **shades of that dominant color;**
- Enhance the whole with **black** and **white** employed:
  — Pure
  — Mixed with the dominant to obtain:

  various paler tones
  various darker tones  } of the dominant
  tinted grays

- Use, in very small quantities, the complementary color of the dominant to enliven the latter (that is, to "bring it out").

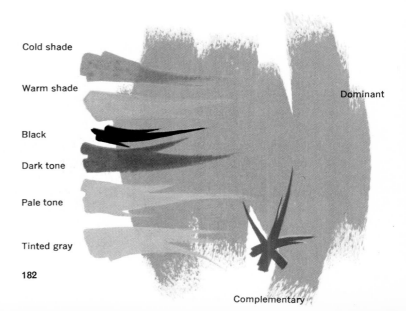

Cold shade

Warm shade

Black

Dark tone

Pale tone

Tinted gray

Dominant

Complementary

182

81

# DECORATIVE PRINCIPLES

## REPETITION

The notion of repetition is a familiar one. It is found in nature and in decoration too, since the very beginnings of art.

## I — PROPERTIES

184. Arch. Door of the church of Morlaas, France.

**1.** Repetition is a **practical method.** The easiest solution for decorating a surface is to repeat the same motif. There is, therefore, an economy of invention.

The motif itself can be very simple. It can even appear uninteresting, but by multiplication it contributes to the animation and embellishment of a surface (fig. 189).

**2. Some methods of repetition attract attention.** An isolated element may go unnoticed, but when repeated it commands interest.

This property is much used in advertising campaigns: repeated praise of a new product, a new object; the repetition of its name, its image, through signs, handbills, pamphlets, posters, radio, television.

Examples: Publicity for movies, books, plays; advertising for cigarettes, beer, hairdressing, automobiles, etc.

A repeated subject carries more weight; it "catches on," like the refrain of a song.

**3.** Repetition can also suggest **weight, greatness, nobility** (like the effect of imposing numbers of men in a parade; the same gestures, the same rhythm, in the celebration of a rite, figs. 190, 193). It helps to give an impression of regularity and unity which is agreeable to the eye and satisfying to the mind (figs. 191, 192).

**4.** It can produce **comic or tragic reactions:**

— Example of comic effect: in films, the repeated mechanical gestures of Charlie Chaplin; in the circus, the "troupe" of dogs or chimpanzees; in the theatre, the repetition of words in comedies.

— Example of tragic effect: repeated lamentations in a classical tragedy.

185. Unusual, impressive alignment. Group of four baboons. The Luxor obelisk, Egypt, XIX dynasty (Louvre).

186. Plaque. Benin art (Museum of Man, Paris).

187. Gothic grill (detail) (Barcelona).

188. Pavement of San Miniato (Florence)

189. Aubusson tapestry. The Open Cage, by Picart le Doux.

190. Procession. Portal frieze of Saint-Trophime in Arles, late 12th century (Museum of French Monuments, Paris).

192. Impression of peaceful regularity. Gothic cloister at Tarragona (Spain).

191. Church of San Michele, Lucca (Italy).

193. Teutonic knights prepare to go into battle in a frightening repetition of lances. Eisenstein prepared his scenes geometrically, he was an architect before he produced films. Scene from the film "Alexandre Nevski" (1938).

## II — PRACTICAL APPLICATIONS

Repetition is one of the most common decorative principles, and is especially effective.

- **Decorative forms using repetition:**
  - Surfaces limited in both directions: the square, the circle, etc.;
  - Surfaces limited in one direction: borders;
  - Unlimited surfaces: backgrounds.

Other decorative principles derived from repetition: radiation, parallelism, symmetry, etc.

## DIFFERENT MODES OF REPETITION

a) Repetition of linear elements:

- Rectilinear, according to:

  A straight line;

  A broken, regular line;

  A broken, irregular line (fig. 194).

- Non-rectilinear, according to:

$$\left.\begin{array}{l} \text{A regular curve} \\ \text{(fig. 195 A)} \end{array}\right\} \begin{array}{l} \text{Open;} \\ \text{Half-open (spiral)} \\ \text{Closed} \end{array}$$

$$\left.\begin{array}{l} \text{(An irregular curve)} \\ \text{(fig. 195 B)} \end{array}\right\} \begin{array}{l} \text{Open} \\ \text{Half-open} \\ \text{Closed} \end{array}$$

b) Surface development (fig. 196):

- On a network of straight lines;
- On a network of curved lines.

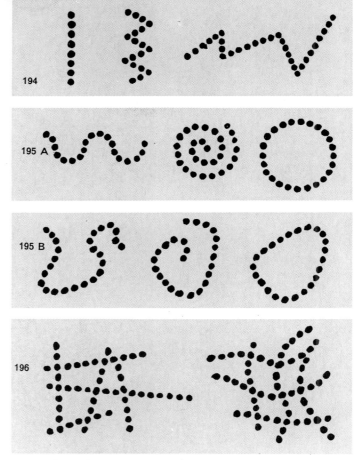

## METHODS OF REPETITION

- A motif may be repeated by tracing; by stencil; by potato stamp, linoleum block, etc.

Other principles of decoration can be added to repetition to break the monotony. They are alternation, inversion, superposition.

85

197. Necklace.
Ptolemaic amulets.
Egypt (Louvre).

198. Gate of Subes (Museum of Modern Art, Paris).

199. Character:
"Diana."

# ALTERNATION

*. . . Alternation has more piquancy and charm, repetition more grandeur.*

Charles Blanc

Alternation, like repetition, is found in nature, and the history of art offers us many examples.

## I — PROPERTIES

Alternation brings variety to repetition. It adds an unexpected element; the interest is renewed with each motif.

## II — PRACTICAL APPLICATIONS, VARIOUS POSSIBILITIES OF ALTERNATION

— Alternation of dimensions;
— Alternation of straight and curved lines (fig. 212, p. 90);
— Alternation of thick and thin lines (figs. 198, 199);
— Alternation of a simple contour and a complicated contour;
— Alternation of line and area;
— Alternation of flat and relief (fig. 202);
— Alternation of motif (fig. 201);
— Alternation of direction or position (fig. 210, p. 89);
— Alternation of values;
— Alternation of colors (fig. 197);
— Alternation of full and blank space (fig. 200);
— Alternation of richly detailed and blank surfaces.

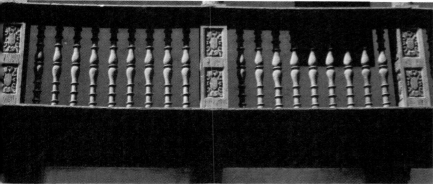

200. Balcony. Spanish pueblo (Barcelona).

201. Frieze of the Erechtheum. (Museum of the Acropolis, Athens).

202. Vase. Pine-cone decoration. Bolivia. (Museum of Man, Paris).

203. Model of a stage-setting. Gouache. Chapelain-Midy.

205. Acrobatic figure with head hanging down, on a capital of the Saint-Rémy-de-Provence cloister.

204. The inversion of values creates a cataclysmal, end-of-the-world atmosphere which was Monsu Desiderio's specialty. 17th century (Museum of Decorative Arts, Paris).

The technique is also used in movies: "Nosferatu," by Murnau: Orpheus, by Cocteau.

# INVERSION

Variety can also be added to repetition by means of the principle of inversion.

## I — PROPERTIES

**1.** Inversion permits the complete **renewal** of the appearance of a form.

**2.** It produces **surprising, amusing effects** (fig. 205), creates an impression of the unusual and marvelous (example: effects of negatives, inversions of value, fig. 204).

**3.** The inversion of a motif is sometimes a necessity (example: playing cards, gaming tables).

**4.** Inversion is also a means of attracting attention (for example, in advertising).

Inversion always adds an unexpected element. It gives **balance without monotony.**

## II — VARIOUS POSSIBILITIES OF INVERSION

— Inversion of dimensions (figs. 449, 478, 486);

— Inversion of position (figs. 206, 209);

— Inversion of values or of colors (figs. 207, 352).

88

06.
reek frieze.
he Acropolis,
thens.

207. The shaded
profile stands
out against a
white tablecloth
and the light
bonnet against a
dark background.
Saying Grace
(detail). Chardin
(Museum of
the Louvre).

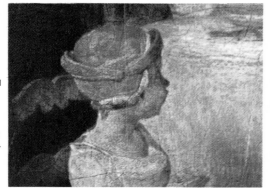

211. Inversion of color and motifs
on the right leg of the child. The
history of costumes and heraldry
offers many examples of this procedure. Primitive Italian painting
(Museum of Decorative Arts. Paris).

208. The reflection in the water renews the appearance
of the architecture. Ponte Vecchio (Florence).

◀ 210. Textile.
Peru (Museum of Man.)

212. Church window in Chalons-sur-Marne.

213. This sculptured tracery is the result of the complex superposition of supple and rigid "ribbons." Bas-relief in stucco. Iran, 13th century (Seattle Art Museum).

Fragmentation of movements with superposition of successive stages.

214. Nude Descending a Staircase. Painting by Marcel Duchamp, 1912 (Museum of Art, Philadelphia).

215. Chronophotograph of young girl descending stairs (negative).

# SUPERPOSITION

## I — PROPERTIES

**1.** The principle of superposition always **enriches** a decoration (examples: traceries, ornamental foliage, fig. 213).

**2.** It can **reinforce** the evocative power of an element (fig. 217).

**3.** It can contribute to an impression of **movement** (figs. 214, 215).

**4.** It can contribute to an impression of the **fantastic** and the world of dreams (for example, in photography or in films).

## II — VARIOUS POSSIBILITIES OF SUPERPOSITION

— Superposition of elements of a different or a similar nature (figs. 219, 218);

— Superposition of elements of different dimensions (fig. 216);

— Superposition of elements of construction and decoration;

— Superposition of different decorative arrangements (fig. 212).

217. The superimposition of candles on a forest creates a dreamlike atmosphere and adds an unusual touch to this scene famous in the history of films. Sequence from the film, "The Fall of the House of Usher," by Jean Epstein, 1928.

218. Publicity for Ford cars.

219. Bas-relief, middle of 12th century (Cathedral of Le Mans).

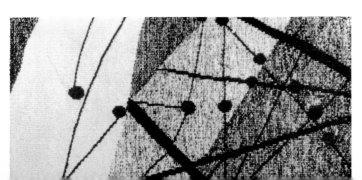

216. Danae (detail). Tapestry by Adam (Museum of Modern Art, Paris).

220. An extremely noble, classical façade given rhythm by vertical and horizontal lines, constructed according to the principles of repetition and alternation down to the last details. The square court of the Louvre, facade by Pierre Lescot.

• The knowledge and understanding of the principles set forth in this chapter are useless if, in their application, one neglects the basic rule of VARIETY IN UNITY. This rule applies to the design and drawing of motifs as well as to the choice of colors.

• **Equalities should be avoided** (in decorations, in blank spaces and in colored surfaces.)

• The study of REPETITION and its elementary principles leads to the notion of RHYTHM.

It may be said that there is rhythm each time there is an introduction of an accidental but **periodic** element in a repetition (examples: balustrades, façades of buildings, etc.)

• Rhythm can be considered a form of alternation.

# DECORATIVE ELEMENTS

## GEOMETRY

Geometry is to the plastic arts what grammar is to the writer's art.

Apollinaire

In decoration the three principal sources of inspiration are: **nature, geometry, and art works** of the past and present (in which one also finds, to some extent, nature and geometry).

## I — GEOMETRY IS A GENERATOR OF FORMS

The top of a table, a box, a tray, a carpet, etc., may be a simple surface: square, rectangular, circular. A vase, a lamp, may be a combination of simple volumes: the frustums of a cone and a cylinder, for example (figs. 396, 409).

## II — GEOMETRY CAN SERVE AS A FRAMEWORK FOR DECORATION

It provides a convenient way of compartmenting the surface to be decorated and, as a result, of organizing the decoration of this surface.

• This method of distributing motifs inside preestablished areas was employed by the Ancients, notably in mosaic flooring.

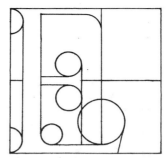

221. Geometric construction of a capital letter. Book of Proportions. Albrecht Dürer, 1527.

222. Geometric forms in "Bizarrie di varie figure." Bracelli, 1624.

223. Roman mosaic pavement.

This system, much favored in Byzantine art (ivories, textiles, mosaics), was also widely used during the Middle Ages (stained glass windows, floor coverings, sculpture, manuscript illuminations.

The simplest "medallions" were circular or square; there were also many examples of "quatrefoil."

Then forms became more complicated by combinations of circles and squares, of circles and lozenges, of several circles, of polygons, etc. (fig. 227).

Later, in the "classic" periods, the method of arranging a decoration on a geometric skeleton was applied to architecture. Façades were made rhythmic by the interplay of vertical and horizontal lines.

The division into compartments, into panels, was also practiced inside buildings, as in the wood paneling of the seventeenth and eighteenth centuries (fig. 169).

• In the field of painting, geometry has been used in every age to organize the over-all plan, which is sometimes of extraordinary complexity.

• In general, one can say that geometry dictates the organization of a decoration inside a given surface.

For borders and backgrounds geometry offers a great number of possibilities concerning the distribution of motifs on a framework — guide lines or a "grill"—which is essentially geometric.

In the same way, the ornamentation of a circle, a square, or a rectangle should be carried out with geometric rules in mind.

## III — GEOMETRIC DECORATION

The basic geometric elements—such as the dot and the line—, the elementary figures—such as the square, the

224. The Oath of the Horatii. David (Louvre).

Geometric construction of the composition:
— The three arcades in the background both separate and relate the three groups: the warriors, the father, the women
— The figures are positioned according to:
  • A dominant rectilinear system (oblique, parallel or fanned-out lines),
  • Curved lines (open or closed);
— The lines of the flooring and walls lead the eyes to the picture's center of interest: the hands and swords.

circle, the rectangle, the regular polygons—, the more elaborate motifs—such as the spiral, the palmette, traceries, and arabesques—can all be used as decorative motifs.

These geometric forms, although particularly characteristic of "primitive" civilizations, have been employed in every age including our own, in every field, more or less prominently.

Note: Geometry very often furnishes both the constructive **outline** and the **decoration itself.**

225. Embroidery.
Breton costume.

227. Compositions of "medallions."
Mosaic flooring, 2nd century;
window of Chartres, 12th century.

228. Pillar of the west door,
1145-1160. Chartres (Museum
of French Monuments, Paris).

229. Church of Santa Croce (Florence).

226. Basque vestry chest, 12th century (detail). (Hernoult Collection, Pau, France.)

230. Calabash. The Cameroons (Museum of Man, Paris).

Diamond points

Pearls

Coins

Serrations

Bezants

Broken strokes

Chevrons

Greek border

Lozenges

Meanders

**96** Scales

231. Motifs in a modern Danish carpet.

233. Gold flask. Hittite art, second half of III millenary B.C.

234. Alcazar of Seville.

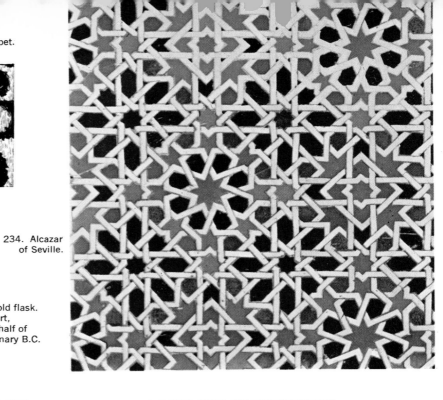

## IV — WHY THIS USE OF GEOMETRY?

• Geometry has sometimes been used for **intellectual or philosophical reasons.** Thus, there developed at the beginning of the Middle Ages a style called "geometrism," the best known example of which is the Album of Villard de Honnecourt, which contains numerous drawings of living forms inscribed inside geometric figures (fig. 96).

235. Benefic green triangles. Saddle cushion of embroidered leather. Saharan art.

For contemporary times we can cite the "constructivist" movement illustrated by painters such as Mondrian or Vasarély (figs. 375, 509).

- There are also often **reasons of a magical or symbolic order,** especially in primitive art, or African Negro art.

Examples:

— The sign ① or ◉, for the Tuaregs, is a protection against "the evil eye"; it is traced in the sand before the baking of pottery to prevent cracking.

— The star and the cross, in Saharan art, are also benefic forms. The triangle is found on all pendants, leather decorations and tattooings of the Mozabites (fig. 235).

— The swastika, in both Europe and Asia, has always been, it would seem, a symbol of the sun, sign of fertility. It is one of the oldest signs and is believed to have existed since the Neolithic period (fig. 233).

In Arabian art in particular, where the Koran forbids the representation of living creatures, geometric decoration underwent considerable development.

But geometry is, first and foremost, used for **visual reasons.**

It is, of course, a convenient system for decorating a surface. It is also a satisfying system. Geometry gives greater precision to the drawing of forms, allows for a logical organization of the design and a more precise arrangement of the elements employed. It brings order, promotion, thought, equilibrium, nobility.

"The square, the circle and the triangle are forms which possess in themselves a sufficient plastic expression" (Kandinsky, 1912, "Le Spirituel dans l'Art").

# THE DOT, THE LINE
## DECORATIVE ELEMENTS

### I — WHERE ARE THE DOT AND LINE FOUND?

- The dot and the line, the elements of decoration, are found, first of all, in nature.

— Flora: nodes and stems, spots and ribs of leaves, the various combinations of stalks and branches, etc. (figs. 239, 260, 416, 495).

— Fauna: the spots and stripes in the exterior ornamentation of shellfish, fish, butterfly wings, feathers and fur (leopards, zebras) etc. (figs. 150, 238).

— Minerals: siliceous rocks (millstone and sandstone) or crystallines (granite); ribbon rocks (gneiss) or lamellar rocks (mica, schist); veined marble, etc. (figs. 236, 237, 487, 488).

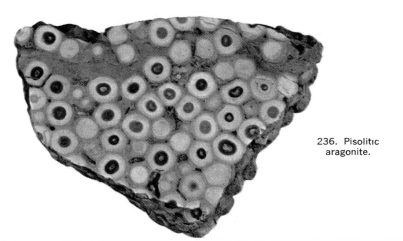

236. Pisolitic aragonite.

239. Gnarls in wood.

237. Agate.

- **Definitions:**

  — In geometry: the dot is the intersection of two lines; the line is the intersection of two surfaces; the drawn line is the materialization of the line.

  — In decoration: the dot has two dimensions. It is a figure of very small size (circle, square, triangle, star, etc.) (figs. 184, 319).

  In the same way, the line always has some width.

## II — WHEN DO THEY APPEAR IN DECORATIVE ART?

They have existed since the origins of art: essentially linear geometric ornaments have been found on prehistoric pottery and artifacts, in Negro and Mexican art, and in the art of the ancient Far East.

The Middle Ages made remarkable use of them (manuscripts, sculpture) (see sections on Borders, Traceries).

Their use continued in the French Renaissance, but they were rarely employed alone and were reserved almost exclusively for borders, frames or for filling in very small surfaces (example: Louis XV interior decoration).

238. Photogram of a feather

240. Bronze panther. Benin.

242. Wine vase. Bronze.
China, Shang period,
15th-14th centuries B.C.

243. Large Cretan Jar
(National Museum of Athens).

241. Bull. Iranian art,
8th-7th centuries B.C.
(Prince Firouz Collection,
Teheran).

## III — WHY ARE THESE ELEMENTS USED?

**1.** The line is a **spontaneous mode of expression:** every young child when first given a pencil amuses himself by drawing lines and dots.

Among primitive peoples, the first representations of volumes, the first anatomical researches into the portrayal of the human body, were expressed by linear indications.

99

244. Lines accentuate the form of the eyes. Female head, sarcophagus. Egypt (Louvre).

245. The dark rod of the wall map emphasizes the gesture of the woman reading a letter. The Letter (detail). Vermeer (Rijksmuseum, Amsterdam).

**2.** The dot and the line serve to:

- **Represent:**

  Example: In the South Sea Islands, on decorated bark plates, dotted lines represented human or animal outlines.

- **Underline, frame** (figs. 244, 245, 303):

  Example: In architecture, the mouldings at the bases of arches, or around the bases and tops of columns; the cornices around the edges of roofs or stories; the frames of doors and windows (fig. 251).

- **Partition and give rhythm** to the whole (see section on Geometry):

  Example: Medieval stained-glass windows; interior architecture under Louis XIV and XV; arrangement of classic façades (figs. 169, 220).

- **Enrich surfaces:**

  In all ages, latticework has been used to decorate backgrounds (figs. 247, 268).

**3.** Characteristics of these elements:

— Precision;

— Simplicity, sobriety;

— Elegance, refinement;

246. Beer mug in white wood, engraved with red-hot iron. Estonia (U.S.S.R.).

247. Plate, 18th century (Museum of Decorative Arts, Paris).

248. The Adam House (Angers, France).

249. Ruccellai palace (Florence).

250. Archaic Etruscan jewelry, 6th-5th centuries B.C. (Louvre).

251. Foscari palace, 14th century (Venice).

— Mystery (traceries, labyrinths, Negro masks, tattoos);

— Magic symbolism (see sections on Geometry, Tracery, Spirals).

**4.** The use of the dot and the line is, in general, determined by technical imperatives:

• In **architecture:** linear decorative effects can be obtained on a façade by various methods of bonding or through the use of different materials (brick, freestone, marble) (figs. 229, 248, 249).

• In the **metal arts:** compositions in wrought-iron are always essentially linear (grills, hinges); studding gives interesting decorative effects. Chasing on bronze or precious metals can produce beautiful linear decorations (figs. 250, 253, 256, 296).

• **Stained-glass windows** use a linear network of lead to assemble the pieces of glass.

• In **ceramics:** the diverse decorating procedures permit numerous effects with dots and lines.

• **Mosaic** is by its nature a "pointillist" or stippling technique (see chapter on techniques: Ceramics, Mosaic).

• **In many other fields, too,** one finds linear or dotted decorations: marquetry, bookbinding (fig. 259), enamel, glass, filigrees (fig. 254), the graphic arts.

252. Conversation between two ephebi.
Back of bronze mirror. Greece,
4th century (Louvre).

253. Merovingian fibula
(Museum of Chelles, France).

254. Filigreed glass. Small bottle, 17th-18th centuries
(Museum of Decorative Arts, Paris).

255. Valencian plate, 15th century.
Spain (Louvre).

256. Black leather trunk, copper hob-nails, 17th century.

257. The Awakening of the Magi. Capital of the Cathedral of Autun.

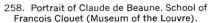

258. Portrait of Claude de Beaune. School of
Francois Clouet (Museum of the Louvre).

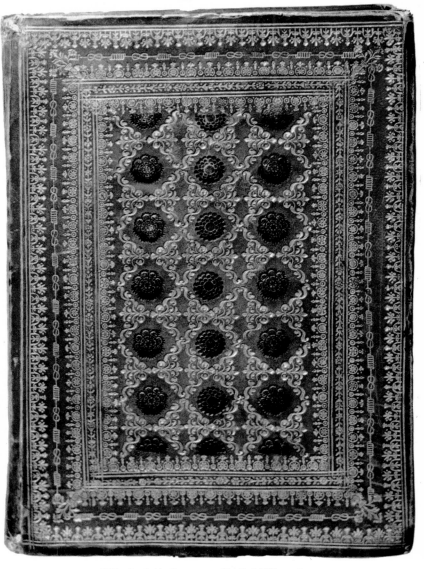

259. Book binding, second half of 17th century
(Museum of Decorative Arts, Paris).

## IV — HOW TO USE THEM

**1. The dot,** repeated and combined with other figures, can become an interesting element in decoration.

One can vary: the form, the dimensions, the value, the color, the intervals.

One can use horizontal, vertical alignments, parallel rows, etc.

One can use them in borders, over-all designs, backgrounds.

One can combine arrangements of dots with lines: straight (horizontal, vertical, oblique, broken . . .) or curved, continuous or discontinuous . . .

**2. The line** also offers numerous decorative possibilities through repetition and variety.

One can vary: the position of the line (parallel, perpendicular, superposed line . . .), the strength of the line (its thickness, its value, its intensity), the width and the form of the intervals between them.

One can also experiment with an interrupted line.

260. Lines and dots in nature.
Drops of dew and ribs on a leaf.

262. Decoration of the Saint-Pierre chapel in Villefranche, by Jean Cocteau (detail).

261. Painting by Mathieu (detail).

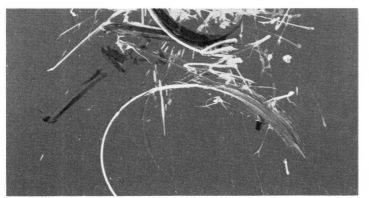

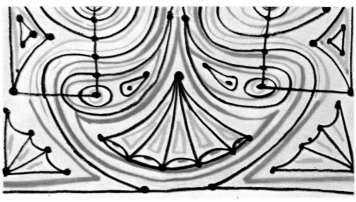

# PALMETTES, TRACERY, SPIRALS, ARABESQUES

## PALMETTE

The palmette is an ornament especially characteristic of Antiquity.

**Definition, origin:**

• The simplest definition would be "an ornament in the shape of a palm leaf."

• However, the word also contains the root "palma" which in Latin means "the palm of the hand" and, by extension, "open hand." Thus, it can be said that the palmette is a radial disposition of elements, that is, a fan-shaped disposition analogous to the outspread fingers of the hand.

• Its form may have been inspired by the lotus, at least in Egypt and India (the lotus of the Nile is a type of waterlily, that of India the nelumbo). As for the Greek palmette, some believe that it arose from the honeysuckle flower.

• The motif can also be compared to the Chaldeans' "tree of life" which, it is true, more often resembles a palmette (or a floret) than a real tree.

> That sacred tree is often found in representations of the gods Ormazd and Ahriman (spirits of Good and Evil). It symbolizes "the eternal rebirth." The fundamental image is a tree with flowers and fruit whose falling seeds give birth to other stalks.

• Finally, it is possible that some of the palmettes decorating Grecian urns were originally a simple **interplay of lines** or of spots improvised by the artist, without any special significance.

263. Flooring in the Palace of Assurbanipal.

264. The most recent palmette: after Le Corbusier's Open Hand, a gigantic sign over the city of Chandigarh (India).

**105**

**Use:**

A great number and variety of palmettes are found in all the decorative techniques of **Antiquity,** especially in Greece. Egypt and Assyria have also furnished us with excellent examples.

In **Western Europe** the palmette scarcely made an appearance before the twelfth century, and was undoubtedly introduced through Byzantine and Islamic art. It is found in manuscript illuminations, in textiles, and in sculpture. Here, it takes a more vegetable, less geometric form.

It was also very much in favor in the **seventeenth and eighteenth centuries,** especially in interior decoration, furniture and wood-panelling, and also in the metal arts (gold, bronze, wrought-iron). Its arrangement then became increasingly imaginative; to a geometric skeleton were sometimes added small, plant-like forms; or else the motif was deformed to resemble a shell; finally, the palmette was used to crown or garland a head. (This idea already existed in Greece.)

**Composition:**

• The radiating elements can be rectilinear or curved (C- or S-shaped, opening upward or downward). These different systems can also be combined.

• The component parts can be identical or alternating.

• The axis can be made visible by using a larger element— a different one, or—empty space.

• The center (or base) can be simply marked by a dot; or a bar, an arc, a small figure (triangle, oval, etc.) or a group of spirals may be used.

265.

266. Textile, late Middle Ages.

267. Palmette in wrought-iron, Louis XV style.

268. Regency table (detail) (Louvre).

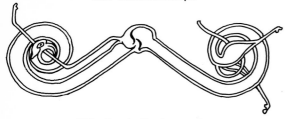

269. Irish manuscript.

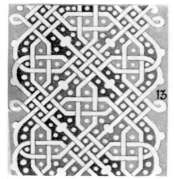

270. Illumination in a psalter, Russian style.

271. Illumination in the second Bible of Charles the Bald, 9th century (France).

## TRACERY

### Definition:

Traceries are ornaments composed of intermingling, superposed lines forming plaits and knots. Always very decorative and pleasing to the eye, they also pique the curiosity, stimulate a desire to study their construction, to untangle the pattern.

### Use:

Examples are found in **Antiquity:** the plait in Assyria, Herakles' knot in Greece.

> The Herakles' knot motif is often found in the decoration of jewels, buckles, etc., and was also thought to possess a magic power which healed wounds.

However, tracery is essentially the characteristic ornament of the **Middle Ages.** It is found not only in manuscripts and sculpture but also on all sorts of objects, textiles, etc. The most curious, perhaps, are the Irish traceries of the eighth century, because of their very "lively" appearance; close study reveals that they are animals with enormously long bodies coiled around each other or knotted (examples: manuscripts, sculpture) (fig. 269).

In the fifteenth century a new form of tracery appeared, the **cadeaux.** These are motifs composed of Gothic letters, with thick and thin lines. They are found in printed books as well as in manuscripts: the Alphabet of Marie de Bourgogne is an excellent example.

272. "Traceries of animals and vines. Decoration in S, 8 and spirals. Ornaments of defense and protection." After René de Solier, L'Art Fantastique. Door of the church of Urnes, circa 1050 (Norway).

273. Shaft of a column, 12th century. Church of Souvigny (France) (Museum of French Monuments, Paris).

274. Tracery of cords. Oratory of Anne de Bretagne, Logis Royal De Loches, end of 15th — beginning of 16th centuries. (Museum of French Monuments, Paris).

275. Strap-work decoration. Capital of the monastery of Poblet (Spain).

276. Bas-relief, end of 9th century. Saint-Geosmes (France) (Museum of French Monuments).

**Leonardo da Vinci** often designed traceries. He used them in decorative paintings, notably in the Sforza castle (ceiling of the "Sala dell'Asse," 1498, fig. 280).

> "He even wasted his time," wrote Vasari, "drawing cord traceries so methodically coiled that one could follow them from one end to the other in the decoration of a circle."
>
> These compositions were called "tondi" or "gruppi di cordi." Dürer later engraved them (fig. 277).

From the **Renaissance to the seventeenth century** traceries remained in fashion; they are found in sculpture as well as in bookbindings, niello, lace and embroidery.

Ornaments composed of intertwining ribbons are called "guillochis."

### Composition:

Traceries can be composed solely of geometric elements: straight, broken or curved lines; checks; hearts, knots, figure 8's; squares, lozenges, crosses, polygons, etc.

Or they can be composed of a geometric framework combined with animal, vegetable or even human elements. In this case, the "living" elements are placed:

— Inside the geometric framework (fig. 219);

— At the intersection of the framework lines;

— On top of the framework;

— At the ends of lines (fig. 271).

277. Interlaced design, engraved by Dürer.

278. Tracery made by highways.

279. Drawing of ornaments. Peter Flötner. German Renaissance.

280. Sala dell'Asse. Sforza castle, Milan. Ceiling decorated by Leonardo da Vinci.

281. Bowl from Saint-Porchaire, 16th century (Louvre).

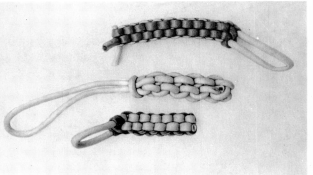

282. Plastic weaving thread has made tracery popular again.

# THE SPIRAL

**283.**
**Ornament on a**
**Gallic bracelet.**

## Definition, origins:

The notion of the spiral can be found in nature in the tendrils of vines, certain animal horns, shells (ammonite, nautilus, snail); in mechanics in the springs of a watch or clock.

The spiral is an unclosed curve which, while moving away from its point of departure, makes a number of revolutions around that point.

One can construct, geometrically, spirals with two, three, four and even five centers (fig. 139).

285. Nautilus.

## Use:

The spiral has been used since the dawn of civilization, often imbued with magical significance. Its form is related to the "water myth" and evokes the shellfish or the serpent. All these associations express the idea of vitality, fertility, fecundity. (Examples: Chinese, Mexican and Negro art.) See figs. 288 to 292.

In **Greece,** friezes of spirals recall the movement of waves.

**284.**
**Ornament for the**
**ear in chased silver.**
**Indonesia (Museum**
**of Man, Paris).**

In **Gallic art,** spiral motifs, S's (simple, double or triple) are commonly found on dolmens, arms, jewels, coins. They were benefic signs (fig. 283).

The spiral still retained a little of its magic power at the beginning of the **Middle Ages** (for example, in the traceries in Nordic borders, which played protective roles). It later lost this power, to become merely a decorative element in traceries, ornamental foliage, arabesques. It then often acquired a plant-like appearance and ended in a rosette, an imaginary animal, or even a bust or human face (figs. 325, 326).

286. Hopscotch.

287. Maori with tattooed face (New Zealand).

288. Decorated tapa
(Dutch New Guinea)

289. Here the spiral plays a protective, defensive role.
Command baton. Dahomey (Museum of Man, Paris).

290. Prow of a pirogue. Carved wood.
Polynesia (Museum of Man).

291. Neolithic pottery.
China (Museum of Man).

292. Receptacle with solar signs and serpents. Mexican art, Mixtec, 13th-15th
cents. (Anthropological Col. Univ. of Vera-
cruz).

**113**

293. Twin capitals. Saint-Rémy-de-Provence cloister.

294. Crook, enamel, 13th century, Limoges (Louvre).

296. Strap-hinges. Church of the Trinity, France.

295. Zoomorphic vase. Hittite art, 19th-18th centuries B.C.

297. Chateaubriand wrote that it took him two hours to go through the Saint-Bertin labyrinth (Itinerary from Paris to Jerusalem).

298. Plan for a museum of unlimited growth. Le Corbusier, 1939.

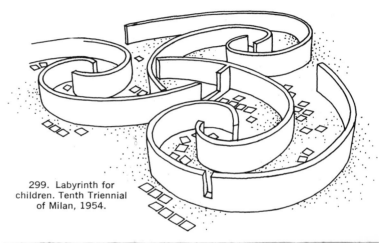

299. Labyrinth for children. Tenth Triennial of Milan, 1954.

Remarks:

**Labyrinths.** Their outline is related to that of traceries and spirals. They are composed of "an infinity of roads over which one comes and goes, taking a thousand detours" (Pomponius Mella) of "false exits which force the lost visitor constantly to retrace his steps" (Pliny).

They already existed in Antiquity. We are acquainted with the labyrinth of Daedalus from the legend of Theseus, who, guided by Ariadne's thread, discovered the Minotaur there and killed it.

They were used occasionally in the Middle Ages to represent the "stations of the Cross" on the floors of churches (examples: Chartres, Rheims, Amiens, Sens). The faithful followed them on their knees (fig. 297).

In the fifteenth century they began to be built in gardens as a source of entertainment.

• **In the present day,** the spiral has not lost its prestige. Not only painters and sculptors but architects, too, frequently use it (figs. 298, 299).

Decorative resources:

The spiral can be used as a decorative motif or as a construction outline, either alone or with other forms.

Its regularity, the repetition of its lines, its flexibility, its dynamism, its strictness make it a particularly interesting figure, rich in possibilities.

# ARABESQUES

The word "arabesques" can have several meanings:

**1.** It can designate **the essentially geometric decorations of Arabian art.** In this case it is a question of ornamentations which are basically traceries, constructed more often than not on rectilinear networks and involving more or less complicated and entangled stars, polygons, etc.

Because Mohammedanism forbids images, geometry was generally used in its pure state, but also quite frequently in association with:

— Calligraphy (writing) which was very beautiful and decorative; and

— Flora (in particular, very imaginative foliage derived from palms). Their curves were freely mixed with the straight lines of the geometric plan.

**2.** When applied to the **Renaissance** and the **seventeenth and eighteenth centuries,** the word "arabesques" corresponds to what were also called "grotesques." During those periods arabesques or grotesques were composed of coiling lines in which were mixed all sorts of fanciful ornaments derived from flora and fauna, the human face, or architectural elements. Vases and draperies are also found, all very imaginatively rendered (figs. 301, 302).

This formula actually originated in Antiquity. In the fifteenth century, some ancient painted and sculptured decorations were discovered in Rome; they were called "grotteschi" or "grotesques" because the constructions in which they were found resembled "grottoes."

301. Loggia by Raphael in the Vatican. Decoration executed by Giovanni da Udine.

300. In this sky, the spiral swirls about and expresses the anxiety of the painter who was soon to go mad. The Starry Night (detail). Van Gogh, 1889 (Museum of Modern Art, New York).

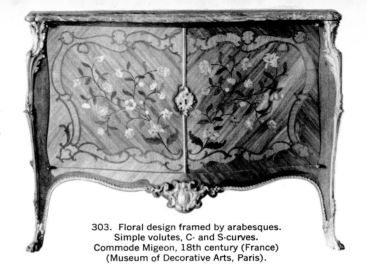

302.
Decorative
panel.
Arabesques.
Berain,
17th century
(France).

303. Floral design framed by arabesques.
Simple volutes, C- and S-curves.
Commode Migeon, 18th century (France)
(Museum of Decorative Arts, Paris).

304. Example of a composition in arabesques. The Lion Hunt.
Delacroix (Louvre).

305. Plan for a formal garden in arabesques. Marot.

**3.** Finally, in **painting**, the arabesque is a **sinuous line** which governs the distribution of figures and other elements composing the picture. It generally takes the form of an S, often an 8, occasionally even more complex combinations. The arabesque suggests movement and endows the painted composition with an internal dynamism which is especially characteristic of baroque art (fig. 304).

# DECORATION OF SURFACES

## INTRODUCTION

In decoration one makes a distinction between:

— Surfaces limited in both directions.

Examples: squares, lozenges, circles, rectangles, irregular figures, etc.

— Surfaces limited in one direction.

Examples: borders, bands, friezes, etc.

— Unlimited surfaces.

Example: backgrounds.

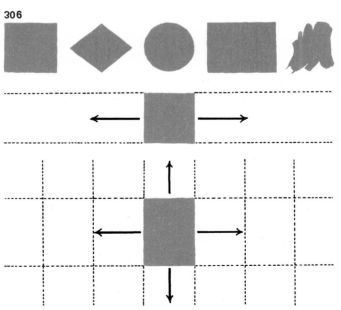

306

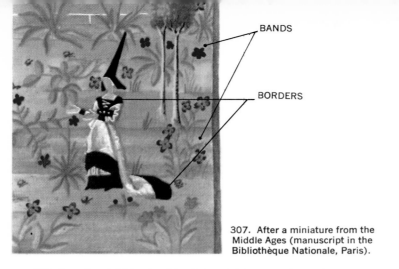

BANDS

BORDERS

307. After a miniature from the Middle Ages (manuscript in the Bibliothèque Nationale, Paris).

308. Iron chest inlaid with gold and silver, 15th century (France).

# BORDERS

## I — DEFINITION

A border is "an ornamental arrangement which serves to limit any plain or decorated surface" (Gauthier-Capelle).

The terms "frieze" and "band," which are often used as synonyms, really apply to slightly different decorative solutions.

• **The frieze** (fig. 190).

The frieze was originally a decorative element of the Greek temple: specifically, it is the part of the entablature between the architrave and the cornice.

One can distinguish between the frieze and the border: the frieze is always "read" in one direction, whereas the border is not. The frieze forms a whole, a complete composition, often of large dimensions, treating a subject usually historic or legendary (in Antiquity, scenes with animals or personages, as in the friezes of the Panathenaea), whereas a border is only a fragment of a whole.

• **The band** (fig. 308).

The term "band" is rather vague and more or less general; it designates a long, narrow surface. In other words, both a border and a frieze are bands.

Usually, bands are used in repetitions, to enrich surfaces (see section on Backgrounds).

The decoration can have a direction (example: the façade of a building) or not (example: textiles).

## II — THE ROLE OF THE BORDER
## (BORDER — FRAME)

It indicates **the limits** of a decoration.

It allows for the eventual **isolation** of a decoration on a background.

It **sets off** the framed element and enhances it.

It can serve as a "passage," a **transition** between the framed section and the background (fig. 310).

It can fill out and **enrich** a composition (fig. 309).

Finally, some attribute a magic power to it (fig. 272).

310. Door, Pézenas (France).

311. The height of the fur border on the skirts of dresses was, like that of the hennin, in proportion to the degree of nobility. Detail, after a tapestry of The Harvest (Museum of Glasgow).

309. Window. Monastery of Poblet, 17th century (Spain).

## III — USE

All civilizations have made use of borders; it may even be said that it was one of the first modes of ornamental arrangement ever employed. The history of art offers us many examples, in the decoration of vases and art objects, as well as in architectural decoration and the jewelry arts.

- **Examples of objects commonly decorated with borders:**

  — In the book arts: bindings, title pages, manuscript or printed pages, etc. (fig. 151).

  — In the tableware arts: vases, platters, etc. (fig. 408).

  We find far fewer objects with borders today because decoration often becomes secondary to substance and color.

- **Examples in architecture:**

  — On exteriors: cornices, archivolts of medieval doors, windows, steps, etc. (fig. 330).

  — In interiors: medieval stained-glass windows, painted cornices (Pompeii) or sculptured wood paneling (seventeenth and eighteenth centuries), etc.

  Here again the effects of color or material have today replaced classic ornamentation, mouldings, cornices, etc. (fig. 167).

◀ 312. Ribbon trimmings. Passementerie.

313. Renaissance chest, detail (Museum Jacquemart-André, Paris).

- **Examples in textiles, carpets, tapestries and ornaments:**
  - In clothing (Antiquity, Middle Ages, Renaissance, etc.) (fig. 316);
  - In furniture (all styles) (fig. 315).

In this field the use of borders has remained very much alive (fig. 312).

314. Copt fabric.

## IV — STRUCTURE AND COMPOSITION

**1.** Structure: every border possesses (fig. 314):

- **A guide line:** this line can be rectilinear, broken, curved, etc.
- **Motifs:** they can be placed:
  - on one side only of the guide line;
  - on both sides.

The axes of the motifs can be:

- Perpendicular to the guide line or oblique to it;
- Parallel to each other and in the same direction;
- Parallel to each other and in contrary directions.

They can also form angles.

- The intervals can be very short, very long or non-existent (tangent or intersecting motifs);
- Borders are often bounded by one or several fillets.

315. Prayer rug (detail). Turkey, 18th century
(Museum of Decorative Arts. Paris).

**2.** Composition:

- The arrangement of the decoration within a border is made according to the principles of repetition, alternation, inversion, superposition.
- The ornamentation of the border is subordinate to the framed section:
  - Next to rich surfaces the border should be sober;
  - Next to a less decorated surface the border should be rich.

## V — VARIOUS TYPES OF BORDERS

Borders may be classified in two principal groups, depending on whether the guide line is **straight** or **curved** (figs. pages 122 and following).

316. Cope of the angel. The Annunciation (detail). Van der Weyden (Louvre).

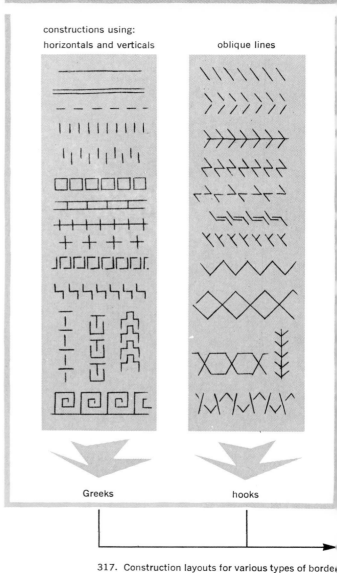

constructions using:

horizontals and verticals     oblique lines

Greeks       hooks

317. Construction layouts for various types of border

constructions using:

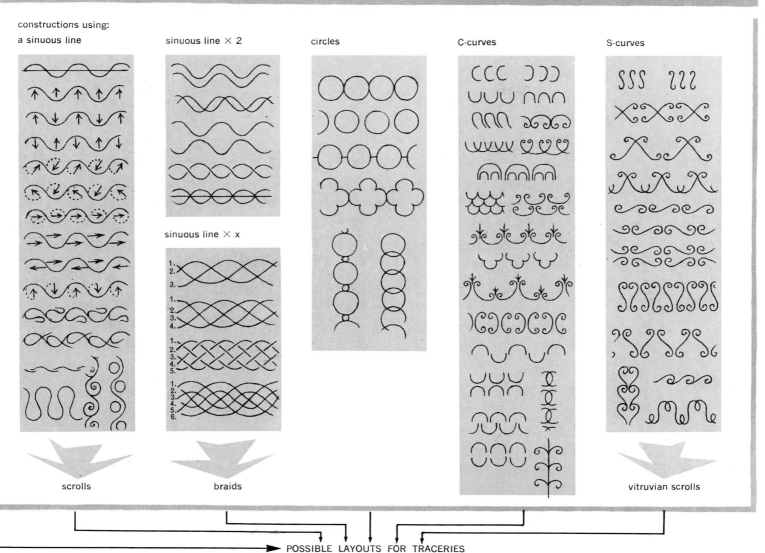

a sinuous line

sinuous line × 2

sinuous line × x

circles

C-curves

S-curves

scrolls

braids

vitruvian scrolls

POSSIBLE LAYOUTS FOR TRACERIES

n pages 126 and 127 are examples of borders using some of these layouts.

318. Design on Tunisian pottery.

322. Design for pottery (Ancient Greece; Medieval Spain).

320-321. Motifs on Tunisian rugs.

324. Embroidery. Russian folk art.

319. Bas-relief. Former priory of Charlieu (France), middle of 12th century (Museum of French Monuments).

323. Lace. 16th century France.

318-324. Borders based on straight lines.

328. Louis XV style ornament.

325. Bas-relief. Church Notre-Dame de Mantes, 12th century (Museum of French Monuments, Paris).

326. Scrolls with heads. 15th-century manuscript.

329. Decoration, Kairouan mosque, 11th century (Tunisia).

327. Molding of a Gallo-Roman bas-relief (Archeological Museum of Dijon).

331. Mural decoration in a house, Pompeii.

333. Enameled motif on a 12th century reliquary.

330. Portal of the church Saint-Lazare of Avallon, middle of 12th century (Museum of French Monuments, Paris).

334. Dragons arranged in S-curves, necks attached by rings. Renaissance relief.

325-335. Borders based on sinuous lines, circles, C-curves and S-curves.

332. Voussoirs of the cathedral of Laon, end of 13th century (Museum of French Monuments).

335. Cornice of the cathedral of Lescar (detail).

# BACKGROUND DESIGNS

## I — DEFINITION

The background design (or all-over pattern) is a decorative ensemble created by the repetition of a more or less complicated motif. The motifs are juxtaposed on all sides.

## II — USE

Background designs are generally used to decorate large surfaces or to fill in blank spaces left by another decorative element:

• They can decorate wallpaper, flyleaves, textiles, a wrought-iron gate, a floor covering in mosaic or ceramics, a marquetry table, etc. (fig. 187, 232, 393).

• They are also employed in bookbindings, illuminations, tapestries, or stained-glass windows, combined with a setting of persons, animals or medallions (fig. 189).

## III — EXAMPLES

Numerous examples are found in nature and in the history of art:

**In nature:** groups of cells, shells of sea-urchins, fish scales, beehives;

**In the history of art:** among the Egyptians (walls of mastabas), Romans (mosaics), Arabs, Chinese, Japanese, in the Western world (textiles of the Middle Ages and Renaissance), etc.

128

336. Tortoise.  337. Italian brocade, 16th century.

338. Turkish fabric, end of 16th century (Museum of Decorative Arts, Paris).

# IV — COMPOSITION

**1.** Remarks concerning the arrangement of the decoration:

If one examines various examples of background designs taken from the best periods in the history of the art, three main categories stand out:

a) In the first case, the decorative motifs, isolated on a background, are repeated regularly. This is a **semé** (lattice) (fig. 339).

b) In the second category, the motifs are distributed according to more or less evident guide lines which have the appearance of a grill (fig. 338).

c) In the third category, very **complex** and intricate motifs leave very little unoccupied space.

339. Repeat pattern. Japanese fabric.

**2.** Construction:

In all cases, the background design requires a preliminary "regulating outline" (or construction network) permitting an even distribution of the decorative elements. (figs. 340, 341, 342).

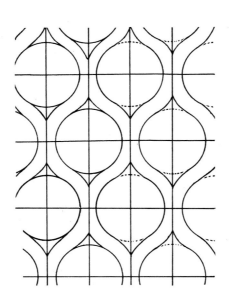

"Grill"

340-342. Construction layouts of Turkish fabrics, 16th century.

129

# V — TYPES OF BACKGROUND DESIGNS

1. The semés (lattices):

a) The simplest semés are completely regular, constructed by the repetition of a single motif, isolated against the background, and placed at the intersections of the construction lines;

b) One also finds, instead of a single motif, several motifs (fig. 343 A).

c) Finally to avoid the disagreeable impression of a monotonous alignment, one can employ an off-center arrangement (fig. 343 B).

344

345

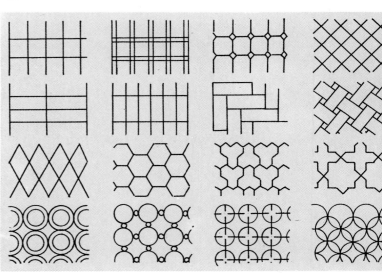

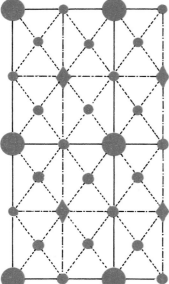

343.A Repeat pattern. Horizontal, vertical, oblique alignments.

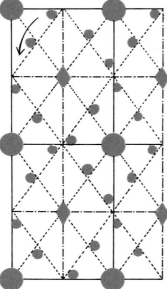

343.B The same repeat with an off-center arrangement of intermediary motifs. A less geometric repeat can be created by various arrangements. See chapter on Animation of Surfaces, page 185.

2. Background designs with a visible grill:

a) The grill is made up of bands (fig. 344):
— Horizontal bands (fig. 347);
— Vertical bands (fig. 346);
— Oblique bands;
— Broken bands;
— Sinuous bands (fig. 348).

b) The grill is composed of simple geometric figures (fig. 345):
— Squares (figs. 349, 350, 351, 352);
— Rectangles (fig. 353);
— Lozenges (fig. 354);
— Polygons (figs. 337, 355, 359);
— Circles (figs. 188, 223, 356, 370).

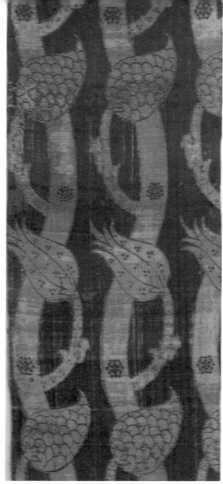

346. Vertical bands. Silk fabric,
12th century (Sicily).

347. Horizontal bands. Fabric, Indonesia
(Museum of Man, Paris).

348. Sinuous bands. Turkish fabric,
16th century (Museum of
Decorative Arts, Paris).

349. The "grill" is left blank. 16th
century fabric. France.

350. The "grill" and the motif blend
together. Moroccan silk.

351. The "grill" is the decoration. Silk
fabric, 4th-6th centuries. Egypt.

349

350

351

**131**

352. Squares. Woolen fabric, 16th century. Scandinavia.

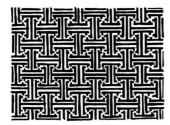

353. Rectangles. Chinese lacquer-ware.

Note: In the category of backgrounds with visible grills, we find the most beautiful examples of the grand, architectural, noble decoration characteristic of the style of the great periods.

354. Lozenges. Tunisian rug.

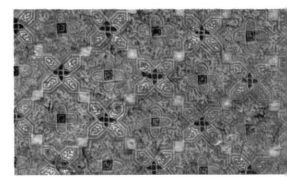

355. Polygons. Background design in "The Annunciation," by B. Daddi, 14th century (Louvre).

356. Circles. Bas-relief. Former Cathedral of Vence, 9th century (Museum of French Monuments, Paris).

358. Fabric with rabbit motif. Gold on blu 16th century (Italy

357. This type of material with a visible grill is also called a "network" pattern. It is constructed on sinuous tangent lines. Turkish fabric, 18th century (Museum of Decorative Arts, Paris).

359. Polygons. Falconer and his servant. Iranian fabric, 16th century (Cleveland Museum of Art).

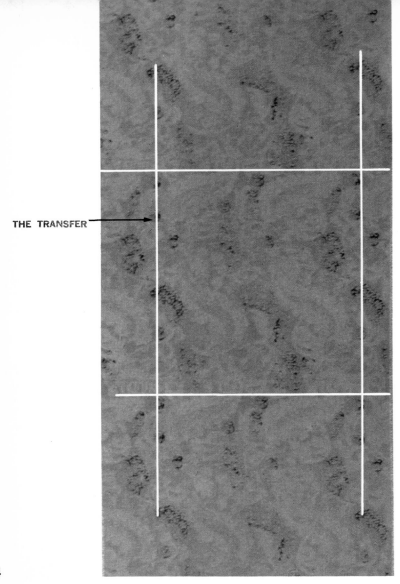

THE TRANSFER →

**3.** Complex background designs:

The structure is no longer evident; a rich decoration circulates in a continuous fashion over the whole surface.

## VI — THE ASSEMBLAGE OR JUXTAPOSITION

The "assemblage" is the manner according to which the transfer, or quadrilateral of the motif of the decoration, is repeatedly juxtaposed to itself to cover a surface (fig. 360).

There are several types of juxtaposition, among which are:

— The straight or regular juxtaposition;
— The staggered or alternating juxtaposition (fig. 361).

**1.** In the case of the straight juxtaposition, the quadrilateral containing the motif is repeated regularly, always identical, in vertical or horizontal rows.

**2.** For a staggered juxtaposition, the transfer, instead of being repeated regularly in vertical or horizontal rows, is shifted from one row to the next, like bricks in a wall.

361. Juxtapositions.

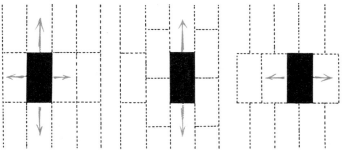

Straight juxtaposition      Alternating juxtaposition

360. Modern textile. The importance
of color and texture.

# TECHNIQUES

## MOSAIC

362. Funeral mask. Mexican mosaic, 300-650 A. D. (Anthropological Museum, Mexico).

### I — DEFINITION

A mosaic is a composition created by the **assemblage** of small, polyhedral elements called **tesserae** inlaid on a **support** and held by a **binding material.**

These elements, varying in regularity and color, may be made of:

a) Natural materials

Examples:

— Stone, marble, onyx, agate, pebbles;

— Mother-of-pearl

b) Manufactured materials (fig. 363)

Examples:

— Earthenware, pottery, enamel, glass covered with gold leaf or gold foil and protected by a vitreous glaze.

The tesserae usually measure from ¼″ to ½″ across, but larger pieces of ¾″ x ¾″ (the Vasarély mosaic, fig. 375) or 1¼″ to 2″ square are also used.

These elements are juxtaposed and imbedded in cement, which is visible between the more or less irregular junctures of the tesserae.

The mosaic support (wall, panel of wood, metal or plastic) can be:

— Horizontal: floors (the mosaics of Delos and Glanum figs. 367, 368);

363. The mosaicist's equipment: hammer, tesserae in a tray.

— Vertical: walls and partitions;
— Vertical and irregular (figs. 144, 373);
— Curved and regular: cupolas, vaults (mausoleum of Galla Placidia in Ravenna, 5th century, fig. 369).

## II — TECHNIQUE

A mosaic can be executed by either **direct** or **indirect** application. Neither procedure is perfect; each presents certain advantages and disadvantages. The nature of the work to be undertaken should guide the mosaicist in his choice.

### 1. Direct application (fig. 364):

This technique is reserved for works of art and requires the artistic ability of the mosaicist.

**Principle:** the tesserae are imbedded one by one in a layer of wet cement; the mosaicist copies or, more accurately, interprets, with the materials at hand, the colored sketch.

**Procedure for making a mural mosaic:**

a) Roughening of the wall: it is returned to an unfinished, raw state and is entirely covered with wire netting held in place by pins;

b) Rough-casting and "dressing" of the wall: a coat of mortar (sand, lime, cement) is spread over the entire surface;

c) A layer of binding material (crushed brick, lime, cement) is applied to a portion of the wall in approximately the same thickness as that of the tesserae;

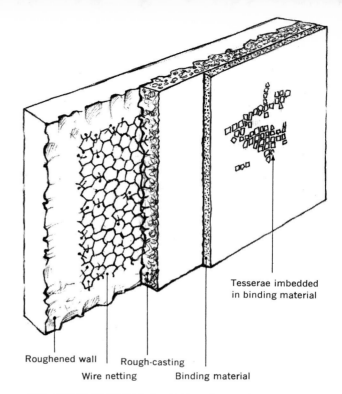

Tesserae imbedded in binding material

Roughened wall    Rough-casting
Wire netting    Binding material

364. Successive stages in the making of a mosaic.

d) Preparation of the material: some elements like ¾" squares can be used immediately. Others, like enamels, are broken with a sharp hammer. More crumbly modern materials are cut with pincers. Some forms can also be reshaped or straightened on a grindstone. Finally, the tesserae are classified by color and shade in appropriate trays (fig. 363).

e) The placing of the mosaic: the tesserae are imbedded one by one in the wet cement.

136

This procedure can only be used at the permanent location of the mosaic; outdoor work or work of large dimensions is, consequently, difficult to carry out by this means (length of time required, need for scaffolding, the possibility of bad weather). Furthermore, the preparation of the support can only be done in stages; the cement dries too quickly for a large surface to be covered at one time.

## 2. Indirect application:

There are various procedures for indirect application, We shall describe the following common method.

The mosaic is executed in a workshop, under excellent working conditions.

The model is drawn in reverse on thick paper. The mosaicist then glues the tesserae face down on the paper. The finished mosaic is then taken to its support covered with a layer of cement.

When the cement has hardened the paper is soaked with water and peeled off; if need be, the junctures are filled in with sufficiently liquid cement; finally, the mosaic is cleaned and sometimes polished (marble pavements).

This procedure has virtually no disadvantages except that of being too mechanical; also, during the application to the final support, various accidents can modify the appearance of the work. Indirect application is usually reserved for industrial or standard uses, such as floors or walls.

365. Mosaic by Bazaine, life-size detail (UNESCO, Paris).

366. Amazons' shields. Roman mosaic
found in Daphne, near Antioch,
3rd century A.D. (Louvre).

367. Mosaic from Delos (detail) (Greece).

## III — HISTORY

Mosaic is a very ancient procedure for covering floors or walls, and has been, through the centuries, alternately very popular and very neglected.

Excavations carried out around the Mediterranean have brought to light fairly intact works of the Sumerian, Egyptian, and Greek civilizations. The great builders, the Romans, left large ensembles. Example: The Grand Mosaic, in the Vosges (57 feet x 31 feet).

With the Byzantine epoch mosaic entered its "golden age." It was used less in flooring — to avoid treading on the faces of saints—than on walls, vaults, cupolas. Colored glass and gold backgrounds were employed to reflect as much light as possible in the narrow-windowed churches. These uncontested masterpieces are the result of a great simplicity of conception.

Examples: in Ravenna, Italy, the churches of Saint Apollinare Nuovo and Saint Vitale (6th century).

After that brilliant period the mosaic art slipped gradually into oblivion in Europe.

The technique was reborn in the twelfth century; in Sicily, the Palatine Chapel in Palermo and the Duomo of Monreale, and, in Venetia, Torcello Cathedral are decorated with remarkable works (figs. 417, 420).

Finally, in Venice itself the ornamentation of San Marco is due to a school of highly reputed mosaicists (13th century).

368. Mosaic from Glanum (France). Greek and scroll borders. The central part of the panel, a true picture called the "emblema," was often made in Greece, then transported and fitted into place within the geometric motifs of the frame.

◄ 369. Galla Placidia. Ravenna.

370. Detail of flooring, 12th century (?).
San Marco basilica (Venice).

371. Archer. Cathedral of Lescar,
12th century (France).

**139**

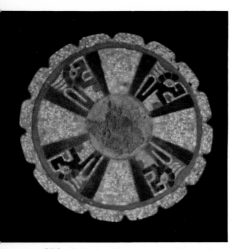

372. Belt buckle worn by high digni-
taries. Decoration: four fire serpents.
Mexico, Maya-Toltec civilization, 987-
1185 (Anthropological Museum
Mexico).

In the fifteenth century the facility of the mosaicists increased, a liking for technical prowess became dominant; and the use of colors excessive (several thousand shades); mosaic attempted to imitate painting and thus lost the qualities exclusive to it.

In our time, after several centuries of neglect, mosaic is again popular. Invigorated by new techniques, it is used as a protective and decorative covering. It is found in many recent architectural achievements (figs. 374, 375).

373. A mosaic of diverse materials covers the complicated form of the support. Spire of the Church of the Sagrada Familia (detail). Gaudi (Barcelona).

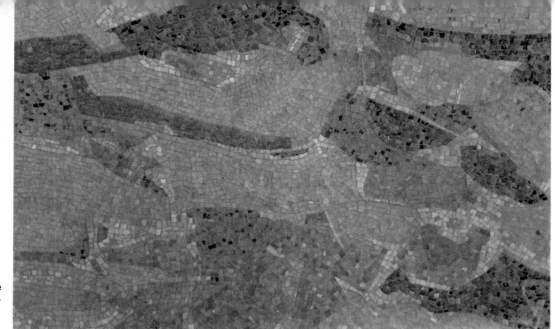

374. Mosaic by Bazaine
(detail) (UNESCO, Paris).

375. Mosaic by Vasarély
(detail), for a modern
building, rue Camou, Paris.

# CERAMICS

## I — DEFINITION

Ceramics is the art of making and decorating articles of all kinds, aesthetic or utilitarian, of baked clay.

Clay is an earthy material which has the property of becoming plastic when moist, and hard when baked or fired.

There are many methods of ceramic manufacture. The most "artistic" processes, which are essentially manual, are **modeling** and **turning.**

## II — MANUFACTURE

**1.** The tools (figs. 376 and 377).

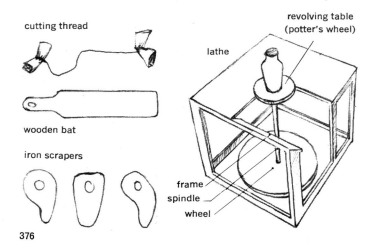

cutting thread

wooden bat

iron scrapers

lathe

revolving table
(potter's wheel)

frame
spindle
wheel

376

377. The potter at work.

**2.** Preparation of the clay: in the state that it is delivered to the potter, clay is not usable; it must be *pounded* and *"pugged"* to make it soft and homogeneous. To conserve it, it is formed into a cube and wrapped in a wet cloth to maintain its humidity.

**3.** Fashioning an object with rolls of clay (example: a pitcher, fig. 378).

a) **The base** is formed of a ball of clay flattened into a cake.

b) **The sides** are formed by tiers of clay rolls glued together with slip (clay in a liquid state) (fig. 379).

— To make a cylindrical form the rolls are placed evenly on top of each other;

— To make a widening-out form each roll is placed slightly outside the preceding row;

— To make a narrowing form each row is placed slightly inside the preceding row.

When the object is completed it is tapped with a bat to strengthen its surface.

c) **Placing the handle:** a roll of clay is attached with slip, making sure that it adheres perfectly (any cavity where air could remain would cause it to break during the firing); the points of contact are reinforced with additional clay.

Thick forms should be sought in preference to thin, and the handle should be placed in such a way that the object is convenient to use (passage of the hand in the hole, good distribution of weight) (fig. 380).

d) **The spout** should not have a complicated form. The best solution is undoubtedly a half-cylinder, attached to the neck of the receptacle with small curvilinear triangles of clay (fig. 381).

378. Preparing a roll of clay.

379. Fashioning a piece of pottery with rolls of clay.

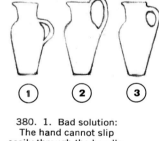

380. 1. Bad solution: The hand cannot slip easily through the handle.
2. Bad solution: the overly large handle does not relate to the general form.
3. Good solution: convenience of use, continuity of line.

381. Forming the spout.

**143**

382. Working a piece on the potter's wheel.

383. Polishing the dried work with a scraper, by following the contours.

384. The kiln.

**4.** Fashioning an object by turning:

a) On the revolving wheel coated with slip and turning rapidly, the ball of clay is first carefully centered;

b) the clay is then raised into the form of a sugar loaf by pressing on the lower part of the ball;

c) At the top, using the thumbs, a hole is pierced and gradually enlarged to form a rim;

d) By pulling this rim upward, a cylinder is made which will form the sides of the object.

The left hand, placed inside the cylinder, pushes out the parts which are to be rounded, while the right hand follows the movement on the outside (fig. 382).

**5.** The object is allowed to dry and is then polished (fig. 383).

Finally, the work is placed in a kiln to be baked (fig. 384).

In industry many articles are manufactured by **casting** or **molding**.

144

## III — DECORATION

**1.** An **engraved decoration** is executed before baking, with a pointed object (figs. 243, 385).

On prehistoric potteries, we find decorations made with the fingernail, or by imprinting with:

— the rounded end of a stick;

— a pointed object;

— the edge of a shell, etc.

**2. Brilliant, transparent coatings** (with a lead base), or "glazes" (fig. 57):

a) The term "glaze" is sometimes restricted to a very thin coating which covers potteries ordinarily called "glazed."

b) A thicker coating is used on stoneware and porcelain.

These glazes are generally used on attractive materials which do not need to be disguised by opaque coverings.

**3. Colored decorations,** through the simple use of different clays, or by decorating with slip (liquid clay).

Different colors of slip can be obtained from the various types of earth available (ochers, reds, whites, blacks).

It is applied to the object to be decorated:

— with a brush;

— by trails or drops (using a paper horn like the one used for decorating pastry);

— by dipping (plunging the object into a receptacle containing the liquid clay);

— by spraying.

385. Pot. Incised decoration.

Scraping can be done afterwards to reveal the basic color (cf. scratchboard).

**4. Decorations using coloring products:** these products have a base of metallic powders or oxides (examples: cobalt oxide for blues, chromium oxide for greens, etc.).

According to the nature of the work and the results sought, the dyes are applied:

— on an unbaked or baked object;

— under transparent varnish, in it or over it;

— with a brush, by dipping or spraying.

**145**

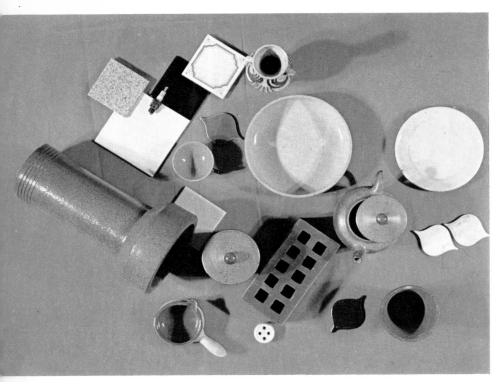

386. A few examples of practical or decorative ceramic objects. Brick; Flower pot; stoneware pipe; porcelain electric outlet and spark-plug; tiles in stoneware, faience and porcelain; faience plate; various receptacles. Ceramics are also used today in the making of turbo-reactor blades, rocket and space capsule parts, etc.

## IV — DIFFERENT CATEGORIES OF CERAMIC PRODUCTS (fig. 386)

There are two principal categories depending on:
— the **composition** of the earth;
— the **firing temperature.**

### 1. Soft paste potteries

a) *Characteristics:*
— Their earth contains clay and sand;
— They fire at low temperature (under 1800° F.);
— They are opaque;
— They can be scratched by steel;
— Broken fragments are dull;
— Their glaze merely covers the paste without being part of it.

b) *Different types*
— Simple terra cotta: not covered with a varnish and thus porous (bricks, flower pots);
— Varnished pottery: covered with a brilliant, transparent varnish having a lead base (kitchenware, saucepans, pots);
— Faience: enameled pottery covered with an opaque varnish having a tin base.

### 2. Hard paste potteries

a) *Characteristics:*
— Their earth contains clay, quartz, and a fusible rock: feldspar;
— They fire at high temperatures (between 2300° F. and
— 2600° F.);
— They can be translucent or not;
— They cannot be scratched by steel;
— Broken fragments are shiny;
— Their glaze is part of the paste.

b) *Different types*
— Opaque stoneware (useful objects: pots, jugs, decorative objects, tiles, etc.);
— Translucent porcelain (dishes, light switches, etc.).

# V — HISTORY

Ceramics has undoubtedly been one of the most widely employed crafts in all ages.

**1.** In **Antiquity:** the Egyptians and Assyrians used ceramics for practical objects, statuettes, and even as decorative facings in architecture (examples in Susa: winged bulls, the frieze of the archers; frieze of the lions in the palace of Artaxerxes II, Mnemon, fig. 387).

The Greeks gave it a preponderant place. The most beautiful works are found in the families of vases with geometric designs (16th-10th centuries B.C.), the vases with black figures (amphorae made in Corinth or Athens around the 6th century), and the vases with red figures (circa 530 to 400 B.C.) (fig. 388).

And, finally, we may cite the Etruscan "Bucchero nero," characteristic black pottery with raised figures (fig. 389).

388. Greek black-figure vase (Louvre).

389. Bucchero nero. Etruscan amphora (Louvre).

**2.** The **Orient,** where ceramics flourished, has bequeathed us many beautiful examples, both from the technical and the decorative point of view.

Examples:

— In Persia, fifth century B.C., pottery furnishings, interior and exterior facings of palaces, mosques, and caravanseries;

— In China, seventeenth and eighteenth centuries, vases of great variety.

390. Vase.
Iranian art,
17th century
(Foroughi Coll.,
Teheran).

391. Bowl.
Iranian art,
9th century
(Foroughi Coll.,
Teheran).

392. Decanter
with lustre
decoration.
Iran, circa
1200 (Kofler
Truniger Coll.,
Lucerne).

**148**

393. Tiling. Turkey, 17th century
(Museum of Decorative Arts, Paris)

394. Vase.
China,
Ming Dynasty,
reign of Wan-li,
1573-1619
(Guimet
Museum, Paris).

395. Vase,
China,
Ts'ing Dynasty,
reign of
Kien-Long,
1736-1795
(Guimet
Museum, Paris).

**149**

**3.** In the **West,** ceramics became widespread with the advent of the Middle Ages.

### In the Middle Ages:

— In Spain: the facings of the Alhambra of Granada, the potteries of Valencia, and, in the fourteenth and fifteenth centuries, the faiences with a metallic reflection of Majorca (Balearic Islands) (figs. 396, 398);

— In France: various objects and tiling in secular or religious buildings (fig. 397);

— In Italy: the ceramics of Faenza (hence the word faience), Urbino, Pesaro, etc. (figs. 399, 400, 401).

### In the Renaissance:

— In Italy: the enameled sculpture of Lucca della Robbia (15th century);

— In France: the works decorated with natural, molded elements by Bernard Palissy (16th century), the manufacturing centers of Saint-Porchaire and Oiron, the workshops of Rouen (figs. 402, 279).

### In the seventeenth century:

— In Holland: the Delft tiles.

### In the eighteenth century:

— Large manufactories in France in Nevers, Rouen, Moustiers, Strasbourg, Marseilles, Sèvres (figs. 403 to 408).

**In the twentieth century:** painters like Picasso in Vallauris, Braque and Lurçat have contributed to the expansion of ceramics (figs. 409, 410, 411).

396. Vase. Valencia, 16th century (Louvre).

397. Floor tiles from Semur-en-Auxois, 14th century (Museum of Decorative Arts, Paris).

398. Platter. Valencia,
15th century (Louvre).

400. Plate. Faenza (Louvre).

401. Vase. Urbino (Louvre).

399. Ewer and basin, early 16th century.
(Deruta, Italy (Louvre).

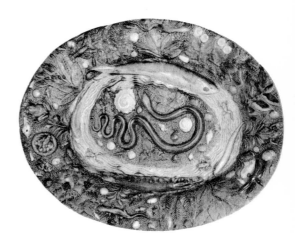

402. Platter, Bernard Palissy
style (Louvre).

**151**

403. Large decorative platter. Bérain. Moustiers
(Museum of Decorative Arts, Paris).

403

404. Plate. Fish decoration. Marseilles
(Museum of Decorative
Arts, Paris).

404

406. Pitcher. Nevers
(Museum of Decorative
Arts, Paris).

407. Salt cellars.
Sèvres porcelain.

405. Platter.
Strasbourg,
Joseph Hamong period
(Museum of Decorative Arts, Paris).

405

408. Platter. Rouen (Museum
of Decorative Arts, Paris).

410. Plate. Lurçat

411. Contemporary Pottery. Derval.

409. Vase. Picasso.

**153**

412. Trees, Reflections in the water.

413. Siren-bird. Detail of
a tapestry by Lurçat.

# 4. IMAGINATION

— **Introduction**
— **The Tree**
— **The Forest**
— **The Fantastic Bird**
— **Insects**
— **Mushrooms**
— **Other Sources of Inspiration — Animation
of Surfaces**

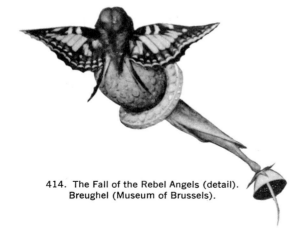

414. The Fall of the Rebel Angels (detail).
Breughel (Museum of Brussels).

415. Panel on a chest: Triumph of Julius Caesar. School of
Paolo Uccello (detail) (Museum of Decorative Arts, Paris).

# INTRODUCTION

> People always claim that imagination is the faculty of *forming* images. To the contrary, it is rather the faculty of *deforming* images furnished by the perception . . . of *changing* the images.
>
> Gaston Bachelard

**To imagine is, in many cases, to remember;** and so the drawing of the imaginary is, in some respects, related to the drawing from memory. In drawing a street scene one calls on visual memories stored up under various circumstances: one selects and organizes them and tries to put them to the best use in a picturesque setting where grouped or isolated personages move about.

The exactitude of the drawing, the values and colors, the anecdotal realism of postures and gestures can give an illusion of life. But to achieve this result it is necessary to have seen well, above all to have observed well.

The qualities developed by observation drawing facilitate the imagination's work. Nature sketches, documentary studies are useful, as are engravings, the works of the masters, and photographs. An oral or written description can orient the visual memory just as a musical background can create a "poetic atmosphere."

In this elaboration in which visual memory plays an important role, the imagination remains rather passive; however, it can become active and creative.

**To imagine is thus to create,** to represent what does not exist; but as the imagination cannot create from nothing, it modifies and combines already existing images. To create an extraordinary bird is to change partially the forms and the values, the colors and the quality of the plumage of a real and well-defined bird. These transpositions are facilitated by applying the principles of color harmony and composition acquired in decoration.

The imaginative drawing is no longer the materialization of a memory, but an **original creation,** which borrows from reality yet does not copy it.

The imaginative drawing employs the traditional techniques of the pencil, gouache, scratchboard and linoleum block; it also allows the use of more special treatments such as collages of papers or textiles, seeds or feathers, bark or twigs, etc.

It is thus a complete exercise, an activity of synthesis; it stimulates the memory and the creative faculties; it makes use of observation and decoration; it develops technical skills and a sense of texture; it can illustrate a text or an idea; it opens the way to the fantastic and poetic.

In the following chapters we shall study the tree and a few secondary themes related to it: the forest, undergrowth, birds and insects. We shall see how they can be methodically developed in the different directions of *realism*, of *decoration*, of the *fantastic*, without neglecting acquired knowledge and without alienating the liberty of creation.

## HISTORY

The theme of the tree appeared very early in the history of art. Sculpted, painted, sometimes represented in mosaic or stained glass, it has survived fashions, and today we find it in drawings from nature and in certain forms of decoration such as tapestries. Its use, constantly renewed, can be explained by several reasons.

In the beginnings of time, man found the tree to be a means of assuring his existence: he ate its fruit; he cut its branches to make arms, fire and shelter. Thus, the oldest images and books devote a large place to it, quickly relating it to religious beliefs.

The **Hebrews** venerated a sacred tree, the date-palm; while the worship of god-trees was spreading around the Mediterranean.

Among the **Greeks** Athena was primarily the goddess of the olive tree, Dionysus was the god of the vine, and the oak symbolized Zeus.

The **Romans** honored Silvanus and Faunus, woodland gods; the **Gauls,** other sylvan divinities.

Examples abound in the histories of extinct civilizations; they are still found in more or less related forms among certain peoples of Asia who see in the tree an ancestor, like the Tagals of the Philippines, the descendants of bamboo.

416. Trees in the mist.
". . . Great trees with black boughs . . ." (Gerard de Nerval).

157

For the **Christians,** Paradise is a garden with "...every tree that is pleasant to the sight, and good for food" (Genesis); among them are the Tree of Life and the Tree of the Knowledge of Good and Evil. The Tree of Jesse represents the family tree of Christ (figs. 419, 421).

Although **religious reasons** explain the theme of the tree in periods where faith was very strong, as in the Middle Ages, they are not sufficient to justify its presence in generally more recent secular works.

**Plastic reasons** played and still play an important role. Because of the variety of its forms, values, colors and textures, the tree offers an infinity of decorative resources, adaptable to all formats, all frames, all techniques. Furthermore, it suggests a place, a climate, and thus serves as a setting for outdoor scenes, of which the history of art offers us so many examples.

418. Tree in an Annunciation to the Shepherds. Miniature from Les Heures de Charles d'Angoulême, detail (Bibliothèque Nationale, Paris).

417. Tree of life with lions. Mosaic. Palatine Chapel of Palermo.

419. Tree of Jesse. Embroidery ▶ (Historical Museum of Textiles, Lyon).

420. The Tree of the Temptation.
The original sin. Mosaic in the
Palatine Chapel of Palermo.

421. Tree of Jesse. Psalter of Ingeborg of Denmark, also
called "of Saint Louis" (Condé Museum, Chantilly, France).

422. The Annunciation (detail). Leonardo da Vinci
(Uffizi Gallery, Florence).

## I — CHOICE OF A FORM THAT WILL DETERMINE THE COMPOSITION

Before dealing with such a rich theme, before imagining a tree, we must first take an inventory of nature's resources and then make a choice, always bearing in mind:

— The purpose of the exercise (illustration, etc.);

— The available techniques (gouache, etc.)

If we consider only the general form of the tree, its silhouette, we can classify the different types in five groups:

— Tall, slim trees: poplar, cypress;

— Rounded trees: linden, oak;

— Spreading trees: umbrella pine, cedar;

— Conic trees: fir, sequoia;

— Drooping trees: weeping willow, weeping birch.

To this classification we can add:

— Wall trees, trimmed into bands, palmettes, and candelabra shapes;

— Ornamental bushes, which gardeners can trim into almost any shape (figs. 422, 423).

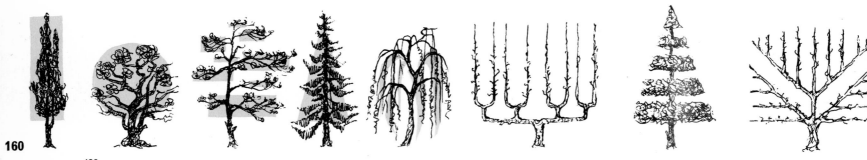

423

424. Virgin and Child with Saints (detail). Baldovinetti (Uffizi Gallery, Florence).

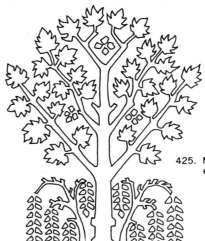

425. Motif of an Oriental carpet, end of 17th Century.

426. Tree symbolizing the earth, in a tapestry by Picart-le-Doux: The Four Elements.

427. Stained-glass window. Bourges.

428. Stained-glass window. Bourges.

**161**

429.
Mountain Top.
Japanese
composition
by Sofu
Teshigawara
(detail)
(Exhibit
Petit Palais,
Paris).

430.
"Damascus"
tiles.
Turkey,
16th century
(Museum of
Decorative
Arts, Paris).

## II — CHOICE OF THE SEASON

When the choice of a tree has been made we can decide on the season: a tree does not have the same appearance in winter as in summer, in spring as in fall. It will thus be represented:

— With or without leaves;

— With or without flowers;

— With or without fruit.

The form and the color of the leaves, the flowers or fruit are likely to vary and, because of this, require different treatments. The tree can also be depicted in the wind or mist, in rain or snow or good weather.

Thus, the choice of the season has its consequences (the same is true of the choice of time of day):

— On the tree's silhouette (example: bending in the wind or blurred by rain);

— On its appearance (leaves, flowers or fruits);

— On the background against which it is placed (gray in winter, luminous in summer, etc.);

— On the dominant color of the whole picture.

## III — EMPHASIS ON ONE SECTION OF THE TREE

The trunk, for example, can be made the most important part of the composition, by its dimensions, by the attention given to its contours or to the branches attached to it, or by an emphasis on the texture of the bark and the irregularites which enrich it (holes, cracks, knots, etc.) (figs. 432, 433).

Or, one can give more importance to the leaves, by employing all the possibilities offered by values, colors, spots, and ribs (fig. 434).

432. Root

"... Is it twisted, pitted, suffering and old!
Are they sunken and swollen the eyes
which are knots in its bark!"

Verhaeren

433. Bark.

431. Basin surrounded by trees. Painting from Thebes,
Egypt (British Museum).

## IV — THE BACKGROUND

• It can be plain, white or tinted.

• It can be divided into sections in a purely decorative way (half dark and half light); it can be divided into more realistic fragments to suggest a season or a landscape (falling leaves or snowflakes, clouds, rain, hills in the distance, etc.)

## V — THE SPIRIT OF THE WORK

All these successive choices are independent of the interpretation. The spirit in which the work is done can be different. One can choose between:

— Realism;

— Decoration;

— Fantasy;

— Symbolism.

• **Realism:** the tree and its background faithfully reproduce reality; all nature observations can be employed here.

• **Decoration:** memory images are not used here, they are interpreted by simplifying their forms, making them geometric, enlivening the surfaces according to the principles of repetition, alternation, etc. (figs. 426, 427, 428, 430).

> If one has chosen to represent a rounded tree in summer, this character is accentuated by constructing the general silhouette within a circle; the trunk and the branches should have a symmetric disposition; the leaves and fruit will be drawn in a simple geometric manner by repeating them, using a technique of repetition such as tracing, stenciling, etc.

434. Leaves. Tapestry by Lurçat (detail).

435. "Living" tree.
The Virtues Struggling with the Vices (detail).
Painting by Mantegna (Louvre).

436. Landscape. Coutaud.

• **Fantasy:** here the tree has only a distant relationship with its species (figs. 435, 436, 438).

> Thus, on an oak trunk, branches of another species can be attached, leaves can be replaced by feathers, the bark by scales, the fruit by minerals.

The procedure is one of deformation, addition or mixture.

• **Symbolism:** the best known example is the Christmas tree (promise of future fulfillment). There is also the Tree of Jesse or the family tree (fig. 439).

**165**

437. Bare tree.

438. Scene from the Polish film, "The Moon Thieves."

"Rendez-vous behind the dream-tree" (Jean Cocteau).

## VI—COLOR AND TECHNIQUE. CONDITIONS FOR USE

• In a **realistic** presentation, the colors, too, should be realistic. The leaves are green or rust-colored, the sky blue or gray, etc.

• In **decoration,** the color harmony is arbitrary and has no relation to the usual colors of the trunk, leaves or fruit.

• The colors are also arbitrary in **fantastic** representations, since one is seeking to create a strange tree, a dream tree.

However, whatever the spirit of the project, which should leave the artist a maximum of choice, it is a good idea to refer to the basic rules of color harmony (page 81).

The subject can be treated in gouache or watercolor, using outline, flat tone and shading; these techniques are suitable for every type of drawing, whether the subject is a realistic oak tree in the snow or an extraordinary imaginary plant.

Treatments using fragmentation and collage are equally interesting, but are generally suitable for decorative or fantastic works only. One can also use paper and textile cut-outs or natural elements of small dimension (seeds, feathers, lichens, etc.). Of course, such methods are not employed in reproducing with exactitude a tree belonging to a specific and well-defined botanical species. A transposition of it is made.

440. Trees drawn
in pencil for
an architectural
design.

441. Bas-relief. Hôtel Jacques-Coeur in Bourges,
13th century (Museum of French Monuments, Paris).

442. The Offering of the Heart. Tapestry (Museum of Cluny).

# THE FOREST

The logical extension of the tree theme, studied in its various aspects, is the forest.

Although this exercise calls upon already acquired notions of drawing, color, and surface animation, it also requires the knowledge of new principles of composition.

To limit the difficulties we shall settle on a certain number of points.

Let us first choose a **season** to determine the silhouette and the color of the trees, autumn for example. Now, for the placement of the forest, of which only the outer border is visible, use the full width of the page. The forest is dense and composed of different species and varying masses which stand out against the sky. The foreground is dotted with dry leaves.

A **wide format** can be used to bring out the panoramic appearance of the landscape, to heighten its effect.

## EXECUTION

The execution is carried out in several very distinct stages.

**1.** The background:

It is divided in two by a horizontal line; the upper portion corresponds to the sky and the lower to the earth; these two surfaces should not be equal nor should the difference be exaggerated (fig. 443).

443

**2.** The forest:

It is spread across a horizontal band and is of varying height, extending downward as well as upward.

The trees placed within these limits vary in height and spacing, some blend together or partially hide each other. The form of each corresponds to a **simple geometric surface**—rectangle, triangle, circle—supported by a trunk (fig. 444).

444

**3.** The coloring:

The choice of the autumn season implies the use of a warm harmony based on reds, browns, ochers and yellows.

Two colored grays of different values and shades are applied in flat tones on the background in the regions corresponding to sky and earth; while the warm tones, brighter and varied, are reserved for the silhouettes of the trees (figs. 443, 444).

Then, for each of the trees, the trunk and branches are put in place, according to their structure; from the trunk, the central element, a few large branches come out; they in turn have a larger number of medium-sized branches which bear many small branches and twigs. This network fills in the form of the tree, enlivening its surface. A color which blends into the general harmony can be chosen, or else a tinted white, plain black, or some dark tones which contrast with the background and give a certain vigor to the whole composition (fig. 445).

**4.** The leaf-strewn ground:

In the lower portion of the picture the earth is scattered with leaves, whose distribution, dimensions and forms should be as varied as possible. Some of the leaves can be decorated with ribs, serrations, spots, lines and dots applied directly with a brush (fig. 445).

The use of warm colors assures the **chromatic unity** of the general composition.

Although conceived from a single plan this decorative representation of a forest can be the basis for extremely varied interpretations, through the outlines of the forms, the choice of details, and the atmospheric coloring. But, whatever these may be, and however much they may express the artist's individual personality, a few general conclusions can still be drawn.

To be properly balanced the composition should have **rich zones,** like the ground covered with a carpet of leaves, and **plainer areas** such as the sky, so that each sets off the other. In the middle section, the frieze of trees provides the transition, the "passage" between the upper and lower portions.

Finally, a very well-defined color harmony avoids mo-

445

notony; it remains rich despite the use of warm colors only.

This principal of **diversity in unity** can be applied equally well to a cold harmony with a green base, such as a forest in spring would require.

Without destroying the initial unity one can also add:

Small quantities of cold colors to a warm harmony;

Small quantities of warm colors to a cold harmony.

**169**

# THE FANTASTIC BIRD

Even when creating a fantastic bird one can find inspiration in reality. Starting with a concrete example the artist proceeds in stages, finally arriving at a personalized result, which is often very far from the original source.

## I — USE OF REFERENCE MATERIAL TAKEN FROM NATURE: engraving, drawing, photograph, nature study.

The reference picture preferably should be of one or several birds with attractive, characteristic forms, and with richly marked and colored plumage. For example, naturally decorative specimens such as the hoopoe or the pheasant lend themselves to more interesting graphic interpretations than would a sparrow or a blackbird, which are too simple in form and dull in color.

This reference can be used in two ways:

**1.** Without modifications:

Without changing the silhouette or characteristic details, one can still create a fantastic composition:

a) By entangling the forms (figs. 446, 447).

The artist draws a multitude of birds whose forms, crowded together, intermingled and superimposed, teem with life in an *unusual manner*.

Examples: Traceries. "The Birds," a film by Hitchock.

446. Birds. Painting. French school, 17th century
(Museum of Fine Arts, Strasbourg).

447. Intertwined birds and four-legged animals.
Pier of the former portal of Souillac
(Museum of French Monuments, Paris).

b) By difference in scale:

Only one bird is drawn, but one whose extraordinary dimensions contrast with a tree or other natural element which is greatly diminished. This **inversion of proportions,** this difference between a gigantic wren and a tiny oak tree, for example, creates a fantastic atmosphere (fig. 449).

448. After a modern pottery.

449. Use of out-scale. The Garden of Delights (detail).
Hieronymus Bosch (Prado, Madrid).

450. Head of an owl.

c) By a "close-up" treatment:

Finally, one can draw only a part of the chosen bird, locating the form on the page according to the photographic principle of a "close-up." Thus, the head of a screech owl, a brown owl, or a horned owl, in which one sees only the eyes, made larger still by the concentric disposition of the feathers, acquires a frightening, almost nightmarish appearance (fig. 450).

So far we have not transformed the zoological characteristics of birds. We will now study another technique.

**2.** With modifications:

The purpose of these modifications is to create the image of a bird which no longer belongs to a known category. One can proceed:

a) **By the multiplication of a part of the body:** the head, for example (the two-headed eagle, fig. 451).

b) **By a mixture of various parts:**

— Of several animals:

Examples:

a magpie with an eagle's head, a peacock's tail, a parrot's wings;

a bird with the body of a snake or fish (dragon);

a bird with the body of a four-legged animal.

— Of animals and plants (figs. 453, 456):

Examples:

a bird whose wings are replaced by large leaves;

a bird whose tail ends in a leafy branch.

— Of animals and human elements (figs. 413, 452, 454, 455).

Examples: mermaids, birds with human heads.

These modifications can also be applied to the plumage, which can be replaced by leaves, bark, scales, etc. In this way we can create the kind of winged phenomena that are favorite motifs throughout the history of fantastic art.

The documents used as starting points in the elaboration of these fantastic birds were precise drawings or photographs of well-known species, and were used with or without modifications to create images of unreal creatures. We can also arrive at the same results without using elements borrowed from nature.

451. Two-headed eagle. Fabric.
Hispanic Islam, 12th century
(Historical Museum of Textiles, Lyon).

453. Tympanum, cathedral of Bayeux, 13th century
(Museum of French Monuments, Paris).

455. Winged mermaid.
Design from a
15th-century bestiary.

452. Birds with human heads,
symbols of the souls of the dead.
Painting. Egypt.

454. Pride and lust (detail).
Tapestry by L. M. Jullien.

456. Bas-relief. West façade,
Notre-Dame de Paris (detail), 1210-1220
(Museum of French Monuments, Paris).

## II — SOURCE MATERIAL OTHER THAN BIRDS

**1.** Technique:

One can **group or assemble** manufactured objects or natural elements such as plants, shells, etc., in such a way that their combination bears a close resemblance to the silhouette and parts of a bird.

Example:

Giuseppe Arcimboldo, 16th century; see also fig. 457.

458. Bird: ink-blot-picture obtained by folding a piece of paper in half. "Spots of ink with the faces of animals . . ." (Victor Hugo).

457. Revival of "arcimboldism." Fantastic rooster composed of an assemblage of disparate elements (shells, barks, jewels, etc.). Taken from the advertising for "Old Nick Rum" (Bordeaux, France).

One can also begin with **blots** or **prints** in ink or gouache made on a sheet of paper which is then folded in two; the damp paint spreads irregularly over the white surface, making unexpected shapes and permitting numerous possibilities of interpretation — outspread wings, startling heads, etc. — which need only to be completed or modified to produce silhouettes of fantastic birds. The results will then serve as a basis for an interpretation adapted to the dimensions of the drawing paper (fig. 458).

> If you study the dirt streaks on some old walls or the slashes of color in some jasper stones you may find pictures of landscapes, battle scenes, imaginative costumes, spiritual forms, strange heads or figures, and an infinity of other things, for the mind is aroused by the confusion and discovers many inventions.
>
> Leonardo da Vinci

**2.** The Method:

When the sketch of the fantastic bird has been completed the technique to be employed is chosen:

— Pencil;

— Gouache;

— Collages of paper, textiles, feathers, straw, leaves, etc.

— Scratchboard.

One must also decide on the spirit in which the chosen technique is to be used. The work can be executed as an interpretation or as an exact documentation.

a) Interpretation:

**Collage** and **scratchboard** are transposition techniques: an assemblage of papers or colored textiles cannot lead to an exact representation of the texture and colors of feathers (fig. 466).

The **pencil** offers other resources: Lines, flat tones and shading.

With **gouache,** one can choose a color scheme having no relation to reality, for example, a dominant blue for the feathers, feet or beak.

**Other methods** can later be used, such as colored chalk, wash-tints, pens, etc.

460. Arabian calligram.

461. Yoke called the "Owl." Sandstone. Imitation of the leather yoke worn by ceremonial players of pelota. Mexico, 650-1000 A.D. (Museum of Anthropology, Mexico).

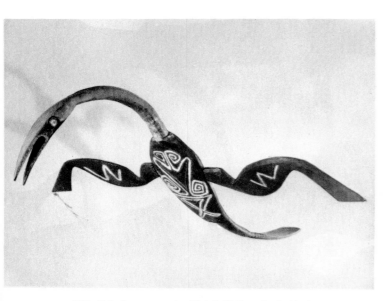

459. Polychrome wooden bird, initiation ritual object. Solomon Islands, Melanesia (Museum of Man, Paris).

462. Bird. Tapestry by Lurçat (detail). ▶

**175**

b) If a more realistic execution is preferred, the pencil, or better still, paint is most suitable. The careful modeling, the close rendering of the plumage will not in the least diminish the fantastic character of a bird whose form and color belong to an imaginary world. A realistic treatment will, in fact, give it even more life, more presence. This impression can be heightened by placing the bird in a very simple setting, which may be a background of branches, a building or a wide landscape with an horizon line, sky and earth. In this way the imaginative drawing enters the domain of Surrealism.

465. Ceramic owls. Mexican craftsmanship. (Janie Pradier, Paris).

463. Manuscript illumination. Gelasian sacramentary, 8th century (Saint-Gall Library, France).

466. Paper bird.

464. Painted, chased metal bird. Mexican craftsmanship. (Janie Pradier, Paris).

# INSECTS

## INTRODUCTION

It is amazing to note that the immense insect world has played only a very small role in the history and mythology of civilizations, with the single exception of Egypt, where the scarab symbolized the most powerful of the gods, Ra, the sun-god (fig. 467).

In later periods, insects are found in the borders of Medieval manuscripts or in some Dutch and Flemish still-lifes in the seventeenth century, but such representations were incidental (and, furthermore, of no symbolic significance). And yet the insect world offers us a multitude of specimens remarkable for their perfection of form, variety of color and delicacy of texture.

## MORPHOLOGICAL OBSERVATIONS

Insects' bodies are composed of three parts. Their only importance here is their appearance and the possibilities they offer for graphic interpretation.

The **head** possesses antennae varying in length and shape, is often very large, has faceted eyes, a buccal cavity with mandibles, and sometimes jaws or a lower portion (bees and mosquitoes) which may be highly developed.

The **thorax** has three pairs of legs and often one or two pairs of wings, whose dimensions, form, color and substance vary from one species to another.

> The wings of butterflies are covered with colored scales; those of the dragonfly are transparent and ribbed; the cockchafer possesses two opaque wing sheaths which are hard and shiny and protect two transparent, ribbed underwings.

The **abdomen,** more or less long and voluminous, determines whether the insect's general appearance is graceful or clumsy.

To complete this brief presentation, a few interesting morphological particularities might be mentioned: the highly developed back legs of jumping insects (crickets); the back legs adapted to burrowing (mole-cricket; a beak on the thorax (rhinoceros beetle) or on top of the head.

To recognize, enumerate and classify insects, naturalists have grouped them according to structural kinships and common characteristics. But within these various categories the artist, who has other preoccupations, can discover infinite new possibilities: for there are big insects and little ones; squat and slim ones; insects with long or short, thick or fragile legs, large or small antennae, thickset or long wings, well-developed or small abdomens.

These highly diverse forms are further distinguished by colors which are varied in distribution, lively or dull, dark or light; and by different textures: shiny and sleek, lackluster and velvety, hairy or smooth.

On the other hand, all insects have two things in common: three pairs of legs and bilateral symmetry.

We can easily deduce from this second characteristic a simple method of construction.

467. Egyptian scarab.

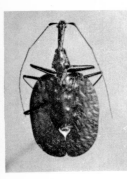

468. Mormolyce phyllodes (Museum of Natural History, Paris).

## COMPOSITION

We can create an imaginary insect by beginning with a symmetrical arrangement of spots of color obtained by folding a page in half (the ink-blot method) and completing this form by the successive addition of elements drawn from nature: wings, legs, antennae, etc.

**The technique must be in agreement with the character of the insect represented.** Thus, a print made with thick gouache would be badly suited to the slim elegance of a dragonfly; it would be more appropriate for the warm velvetiness of a butterfly or the hairy texture of a caterpillar.

The transparency of an ink wash would not be suitable to the massiveness of a cockchafer, but would very well render the lightness of a gnat or a moth.

*The tool and the way it is handled* also contribute to the elaboration of the character of the form. The pen, for example, with its light, incisive stroke would not be suited to the smooth, rounded contours of the ladybird, but it would be excellent for the sharp, aggressive appearance of the grasshopper or the praying mantis.

The insect can also be represented *in its natural surroundings*, alone or in a group, nibbling a leaf, crawling over rough bark, climbing up a blade of grass, making its way through moss or a bed of leaves, gliding on the surface of a pond, hauling a burden, or digging a burrow (cross-section view).

## INSECTS AND THE FANTASTIC

By their unusualness, by the extravagance of their forms, colors and substances, insects are naturally fantastic; they belong to a strange world. Consequently, they

470. Gongylus gongyloides (Museum of Natural History, Paris).

471. Palophus centaurus (Museum of Natural History, Paris).

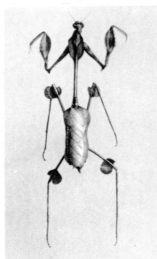

"Oh! The marvel of their sparkling wings and their bodies slim as a needle."

Verhaeren

can be called upon to bring the fantastic into other realms. Some primitive painters have used them in portrayals of nightmares, or in the visions of Hell or the end of the world which haunted men at the close of the Middle Ages.

They are still employed by some artists today, such as Salvador Dali in his paintings and Jean Lurçat in his tapestries, to express certain supernatural aspects of our contemporary world (figs. 476, 481).

Using methods we have already discussed, we can create an imaginative drawing bordering on the fantastic:

— By placing in a normal framework insects of *magnified* dimensions, by confronting them with animals of normal size;

— By putting them in a scene in which they are not normally found;

— By giving them *unnatural activities*, work or occupations usually reserved to men, for example.

To associate insects with men as the fabulist La Fontaine did (for other reasons) is also to verge on the fantastic.

473, 474. Chinese crickets.

475. Stag-beetle.
Sculpture by Etienne Hadju, 1943
(Museum of Modern Art, Paris).

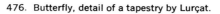

476. Butterfly, detail of a tapestry by Lurçat.

472. Japanese design.

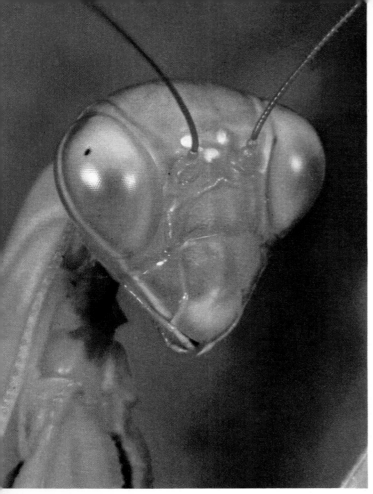

477. Praying mantis.
Close-up of head.

**180**

478. Exaggerated proportions, a source of the fantastic.
Japanese film, "Mothra," Inoshiro Honda, 1962.

480. Personified insect. Grandville.

479. Grasshopper.
Close-up of head.

481. Composition by Dali (detail), ▶
1937 (Museum of Modern Art, Paris).

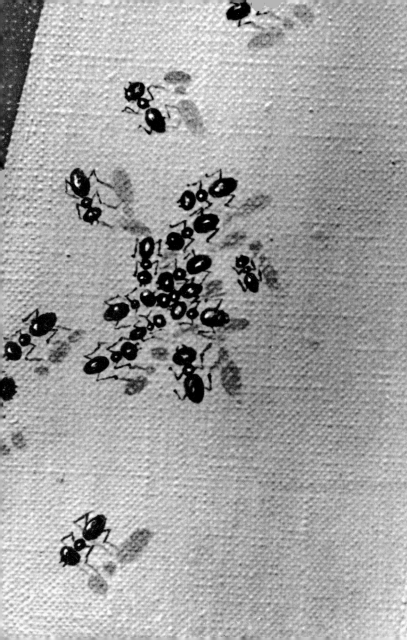

An ant fifty feet long
with a hat on its head,
there's no such thing, there's no such thing.
An ant pulling a cart
full of penguins and ducks,
there's no such thing, there's no such thing.
An ant speaking French,
speaking Latin and Dutch,
there's no such thing, there's no such thing.
Ah! Why not?

Robert Desnos, *Chantefleurs et Chantefables*
(Editions Gallimard)

# MUSHROOMS

482.

Everything is plentiful here, species,
shapes, colors, and scents.

J. de Pesquidoux

## OBSERVATIONS

Before creating an imaginary mushroom we should
make a number of observations from nature or photographs. These will give us an idea of the range of possible
variations in form, decoration, color and texture. These
observations can be carried out in sketches or *flat tone*
("shadow drawing") (figs. 482, 483).

There are many characteristic silhouettes:

— Long, in the form of an umbrella either open (coch-
  erelles) or closed (shaggy-mane);

— Round and squat (boletus) or spherical (truffles);

— Hollowed out in a more or less wide horn shape
  (chanterelle);

— Long and overhanging like a roof (tinder agaric);

— Jagged like algae (yellow clavaria);

— Pitted like a sponge (morel).

The stems vary in length, are smooth, spotted or striped
and occasionally ringed.

The cap varies according to the species. It is sometimes
velvety, sometimes rough; and its underside is composed
of ribs, tubes or rough surfaces requiring different graphic
treatments.

Some species change during their development; the
orange-milk agaric first resembles an egg and then a wide-
open umbrella.

483.

## USE OF REFERENCE MATERIALS

After selecting a type, a decorative specimen is drawn by respecting the character — graceful or squat, rich or sober—while simplifying the general form. Avoid hesitant, feeble strokes and omit unimportant details. On the other hand, the basic contours should be emphasized, by accentuating, if necessary, the geometry of the forms (for example, by drawing some curves with a compass). The silhouette should remain identifiable without being scrupulously realistic.

If the surfaces of the stem and cap are too big, they can be broken down into smaller areas, taking into consideration the natural arrangement of spots or stripes, or by adopting a more arbitrary system of geometric subdivision consistent with the form.

Finally, these reduced surfaces should be *decorated* with a combination of simple elements, lines or dots, employed according to the principles of decoration (repetition, alternation, inversion, superposition).

A few zones free of all decoration should be left to heighten and contrast with the more richly decorated portions.

When the pencil outline has been completed the interpretation can be finished either in line or in color.

**1.** In line:

The preliminary outline has merely to be completed with a pen or the tip of a brush. Lines of varying thickness and strength provide interesting effects.

**2.** In color:

Without betraying the mushroom's character, one can use an autumn harmony with a base of warm colors varying in brightness.

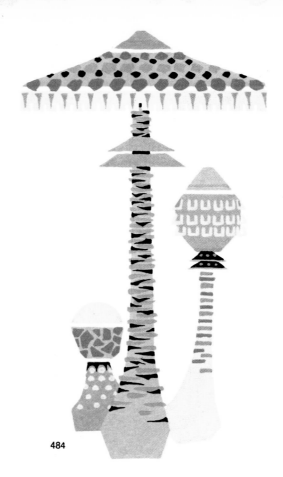

484

The *large surfaces* are painted first, preferably in a neutral color; then the smaller sections, with brighter colors in the same harmony. Repeat each hue in several places, on surfaces of different shapes and dimensions.

**183**

Two examples of fantastic gigantism.

485. Drawing by Victor Hugo
(Victor Hugo Museum, Paris).

486. The Mysterious Star.
Tintin. Hergé.

The *small details* are simply executed directly on the background color with a pointed brush.

The use of a warm harmony does not exclude a few cold tones (complementaries, for example) or white or black. These foreign additions, which add liveliness to the composition, should only be used in small amounts, and at the very end. The over-all impression should be one of unity without monotony and of richness without excess.

This exercise deals with the drawing of a single mush-room whose dimensions are adapted to the format of a sheet of paper, but it can also be applied to a composition of several mushrooms. These should be of different forms and sizes and placed at irregular intervals on a white or colored, plain or decorated background. The principles of drawing, distribution of motifs, and choice of colors remain the same.

The graphic techniques are not limited to line drawings or flat color; one can also employ the textural effects of thick or liquid gouache, prints, or collages of paper or other materials.

# OTHER SOURCES OF INSPIRATION
# ANIMATION OF SURFACES

## INTRODUCTION

To recreate, to imagine trees, birds, insects and mushrooms, we have made use of "documents" drawn from nature, real or photographic. After having chosen and analyzed them, we have interpreted, modified, and transposed them to obtain a more personal result, occasionally realistic, often decorative, sometimes fantastic.

We can also use a different approach.

Instead of a **figurative** document one can create an **abstract** composition which doesn't "represent" anything, in the usual sense of the word; it simply has a plastic value based on the relationship of surfaces, restrained or rich, animated by dots and lines judiciously organized. This composition may be inspired by observations of nature or by the manipulation of objects or natural elements, often simple and small, such as seeds and small sticks, etc.

488. Brazilian agate. "Tiger's Eye."

489. Pile of logs.

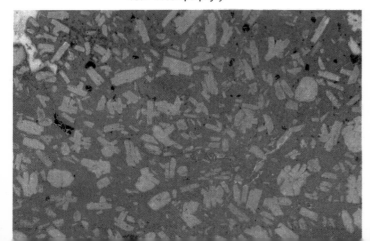

487. Green porphyry.

## ANIMATING A SURFACE WITH DOTS

Place several dozen lentils or other seeds of the same size evenly on a sheet of graph paper. Thanks to the printed lines, there is no difficulty in keeping the intervals regular. In this way the lentils form a very simple background design (semé), but one which we must admit is somewhat monotonous (fig. 491).

A sharp tug on a corner of the paper disturbs this regular pattern. The lentils are shifted around and form uneven groups. Also, the empty spaces are now very different in shape and layout.

The over-all effect is more disordered but less monotonous: **the surface has become animated** (fig. 492).

This very simple operation leaves a lot to chance and the result is often unsatisfactory; it is frequently necessary to rearrange some of the spaces or seed groupings.

After several experiments one may notice that **there are three ways of animating a surface:**

— By unequal masses at irregular intervals: this is the result obtained by chance (fig. 492);

— By unequal masses at regular intervals (fig. 493);

— By equal masses at irregular intervals (fig. 494).

Each isolated seed corresponds to an equal mass; the seeds grouped by twos or threes or more make up unequal masses.

Here the inequalities arise from different layouts. One can also get them by using contrasts in shades (dark or light seeds) or differences in color (red, green, yellow seeds).

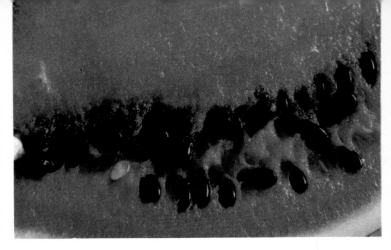

490. Close-up of a watermelon.

491
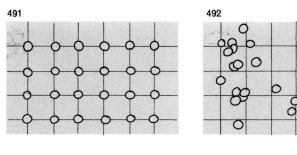

492

493
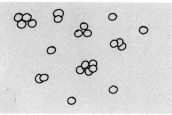

494
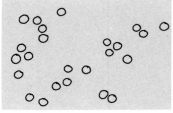

Always keep in mind that the empty spaces or intervals play as important a role as the filled spaces or groups.

These experiments in animating a surface have been made with seeds, the plastic equivalent of **dots,** as they are defined in decoration. They can also be made by combining lines.

## ANIMATING A SURFACE WITH LINES

For this experiment, use ordinary kitchen matches of equal thickness and length. Toss a handfull onto a piece of paper and, if necessary, modify their chance distribution to obtain a more satisfactory surface animation,

495. Wood for cabinet-making.

based on inequalities of "full" and "empty" spaces (fig. 496).

Then copy this arrangement on a piece of paper, replacing each match by a straight line (fig. 497).

Finally, without changing the distribution, modify the appearance of the page by lengthening some of the lines and thickening others. These alterations add variety to the composition without destroying the original distribution (fig. 498).

Such experiments can also be made with **curved lines;** by using equal or different-sized circles, closed and irregular curves, open S- or C-shaped curves, a wide variety of animated surfaces can be created (fig. 499).

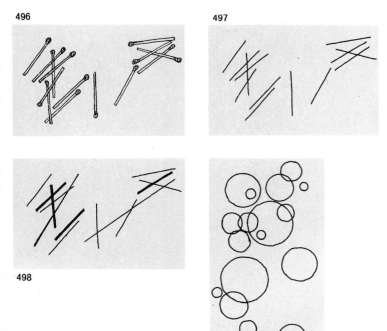

496

497

498

499

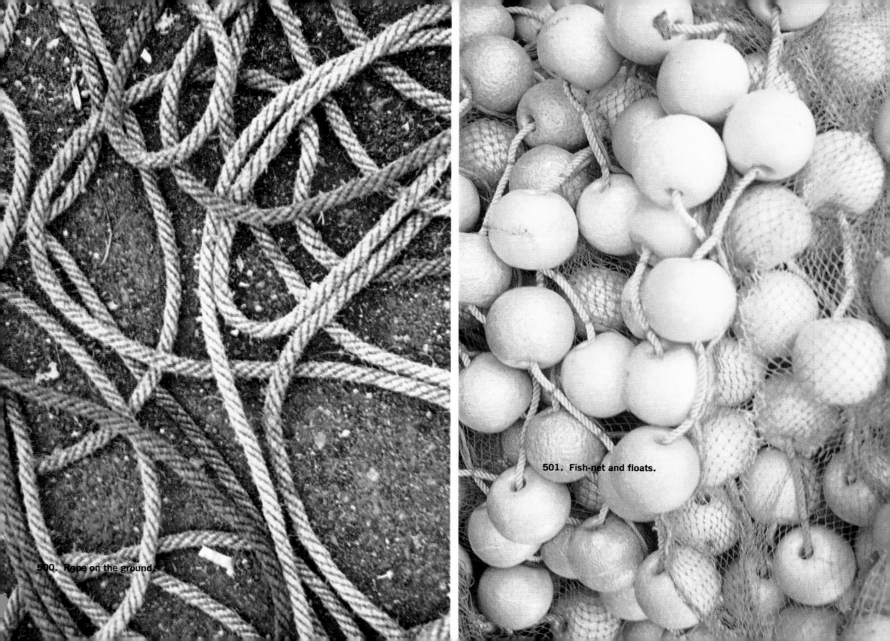

500. Rope on the ground.

501. Fish-net and floats.

# NEW POSSIBILITIES OF INTERPRETATION

The dot and the line, straight or curved, thus permit us to elaborate true "abstract" compositions. They can also be employed in more figurative compositions; in other words, besides showing us how varieties of "empty" and "full" spaces may produce a pleasing design, they can **suggest** or **create an identifiable, concrete form.**

In some cases this operation is very simple:

— A sheet of paper covered with carefully distributed seeds is not very different from the ground covered with leaves; the intervals are unequal, the areas of **separate** or **grouped** leaves are just as varied (fig. 502).

One can, therefore, create an abstract composition with dots and then change the dots into well-defined leaves.

The organization of straight lines already suggests a colony of insects; by adding legs and antennae to each of those straight lines one can obtain a swarming army of ants in action.

— There is a different method of using an abstract composition which gives different results. On a sheet of drawing paper covered with dots or lines trace a clear outline of a bird (or any other animal). The remaining surface is then filled in with thick gouache. On this uniform, dark background the silhouette of the bird stands out; the dots or lines covering its surface thus become the plastic equivalent of a spotted plumage (fig. 504).

Inversely one can begin with a very light outline of a bird and decorate it afterwards with dots or lines; these are *organized* on the bird's surface, respecting and even underlining the profile of the wings, beak and legs to make the silhouette easily identifiable (fig. 505).

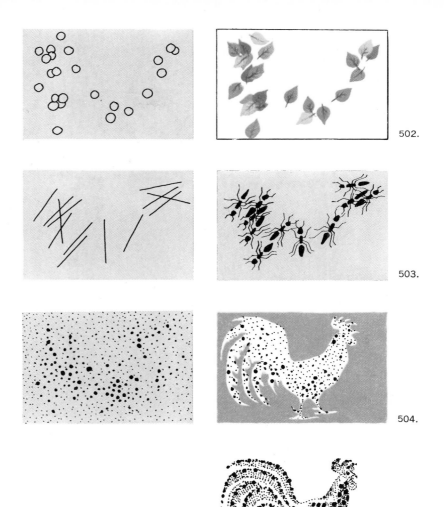

502.

503.

504.

505.

**189**

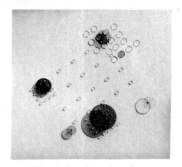

506. Animation of surfaces.
Structures in Transparencies.
Boto (Gallery Denise René, Paris).

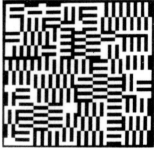

507. Ernst Benkert
(Gallery Denise
René, Paris).

508. Chromoplastic Atmosphere.
Tomasello (Gallery
Denise René, Paris).

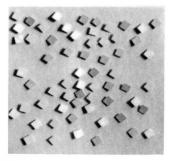

509. Betelgeuse. Vasarély
(Gallery Denise René, Paris).

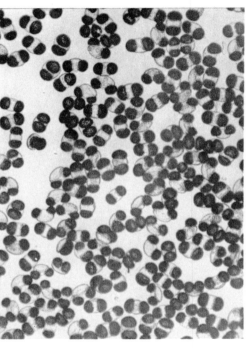

510. Grains of pollen. Black pine
(enlarged approx. 300 times).

Microphotography reveals a strange world whose
forms recall certain aspects of abstract art.

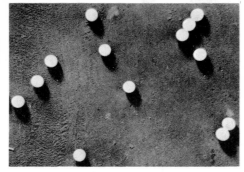

511. Latex, metallic shade. Electron microphotograph (enlarged 17,500 times).

512. Animated Circles. Painting by Sophie Täuber.

513. Oriented Elements. Painting by Camille Graser.

514. Crystals of aspartic acid. Microphotographed in polarized light (enlarged 450 times).

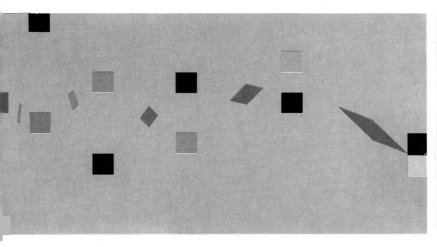

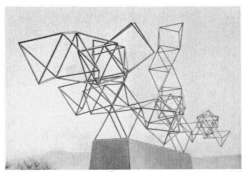

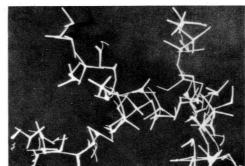

516. Crystals of zinc oxide under an electron microscope, metallic shade (enlarged 30,000 times).

191

515. Sculpture by Max Bill.

# PHOTOGRAPHIC CREDITS

**Baqué :** 3, 9, 14, 19, 20, 24, 32, 43, 46, 50, 51, 54, 55, 56, 59, 60, 61, 72, 73, 80, 85, 88, 95, 144, 156, 162, 164, 165, 168, 171, 172, 174, 178, 179, 181, 184, 185, 187, 190, 192, 197, 198, 199, 200, 203, 205, 287, 213, 216, 219, 220, 226, 228, 236, 237, 238, 239, 241, 244, 250, 252, 256, 258, 260, 261, 267, 268, 273, 274, 275, 276, 282, 285, 292, 293, 294, 296, 304, 309, 310, 312, 313, 316, 319, 324, 325, 327, 330, 332, 335, 336, 355, 356, 359, 362, 365, 366, 368, 371, 372, 373, 374, 375, 387, 388, 389, 390, 391, 392, 412, 416, 429, 432, 433, 435, 436, 437, 441, 447, 450, 453, 456, 461, 464, 465, 475, 481, 487, 488, 489, 490, 495, 500, 501. — **Baqué-Servois :** 36, 360, 363, 386, 411. — **Bonnefoy :** 242. — **Boudot-Lamotte :** 431. — **Braun :** 105. — **Bulloz :** 18, 106, 485. — **Cinémathèque française :** 93, 217. — **Dupuis :** 413. — **Etablissements Bardinet (création Draeger) :** 457. — **Focus :** 407. — **France-Soir :** 177. — **Galerie Creuzevault :** 170. — **Galerie La Demeure :** 66, 180, 426, 454. — **Galerie Maeght :** 111. — **Galerie Denise René :** 506, 507, 508, 509. — **Giraudon :** 2, 10, 11, 13, 16, 22, 47, 48, 49, 81, 96, 104, 152, 153, 154, 201 (Alinari), 224, 243 (Alinari) 245, 280 (Alinari), 281, 394, 395, 397, 414, 419, 421, 446, 449, 451. — **Institut d'Art et d'Archéologie :** 82. — **Institut Géographique National :** 278. — **Knoll :** 145. — **Laroche :** 4, 5, 7, 8, 34, 35, 41, 42, 44, 52, 57 A, 57 B, 57 C, 57 D, 58 A, 58 B, 79, 84, 86, 87, 89, 90, 91, 97, 107, 116, 117, 118, 119, 120, 122, 123, 124, 126, 131, 134 A, 134 B, 135, 136 A, 136 B, 137, 138, 141, 142, 155, 159, 160, 161, 163, 173, 175, 176, 204, 208, 211, 233, 234, 247, 253, 254, 255, 259, 286, 295, 303, 315, 338, 348, 357, 377, 378, 379, 381, 382, 384, 385, 396, 398, 399, 400, 401, 402, 403, 404, 405, 406, 408, 410, 415, 430, 434, 442, 462, 466, 468, 469, 470, 471, 476. — **Naison française (Yordanovitch) :** 167. — **Midi-Minuit Fantastique :** 438, 478. — **Musée de l'Homme :** 186, 202, 210, 230, 240, 246, 284, 287, 288, 289, 290, 291, 347, 459. — **Musée de Strasbourg :** 93. — **Noailles :** 510. — **Photam :** 189. — **René-Jacques :** 169. — **Editions Romo :** 108. — **Scala :** 369. — **Servois :** 225. — **Six :** 150, 477, 479. — **Jacques Suquet :** 215. — **Roger-Viollet :** 45, 110, 121 (Alinari), 143, 188, 191, 209, 229, 248, 249, 251, 257, 263, 305, 367, 370 (Alinari), 409, 417 (Anderson), 422 (Anderson), 424 (Brogi), 439. — **X :** 183, 206, 214, 218, 223, 270, 271, 277, 279, 301, 302, 308, 324, 393.

Printed in France · IMPRIMERIE CHAIX-DESFOSSÉS-NÉOGRAVURE · PARIS.